Fang and Fur, Blood and Bone
A Primal Guide to Animal Magic

Fang and Fur, Blood and Bone
A Primal Guide to Animal Magic

By Lupa

Megalithica books

Stafford, England

Fang and Fur, Blood and Bone
A Primal Guide to Animal Magic
By Lupa
First edition © 2006

Lupa may be contacted at: chaohippie@excite.com
http://www.thegreenwolf.com

Cover by Jim Towns
Typesetting: Storm Constantine
Design: Kid Charlemaine
Editor: Taylor Ellwood

Set in Souvenir

First edition by Megalithica Books, 2006

A Megalithica Books Edition
An imprint of Immanion Press
http://www.immanion-press.com
info@immanion-press.com

ISBN 1-905713-01-0

Immanion Press
8 Rowley Grove
Stafford ST17 9BJ
UK

Dedication

To Nick, for the superior essay and for broadening my magical outlook significantly.

To Jim, for the best thirteen months of my Pittsburgh years, for helping me get through the winter of 2004-5, for being one of my dearest partners, and for the outstanding artwork for this book.

To Taylor, for the foreword, the editing and hooking me up with Immanion in the first place, and for being my partner in magic, creativity and matters of the heart.

I love you all.

Acknowledgements

To all the wonderful people who reviewed bits and parts of this book in its varying stages of development, to those who contributed source material (especially the surprises!) and to everyone who offered their support of this project, I thank you from the bottom of my heart. You honor me by your presence in my life.

To Lyssa, for the first half of the title, and for being one of "all the wonderful people" mentioned above.

To Don, for the excellent copy edit (even though you sided with Taylor on the use of commas).

To Social Distortion, for braving the ice rink and for the song "Reach For the Sky" which was the impetus to get this project rolling.

And to me, for finally completing a major project!

Table of Contents

Foreword

One of the biggest problems that faces a genre in the publishing industry is that particular topics end up occupying specific niches. The niche produces a formulaic format that is relied upon to the point that you have authors beating a dead horse on a particular subject, with little or nothing to write that is original, new, or meaningful. This happens in science fiction, fantasy, non-fiction publishing, and it happens in the occult publishing industry. There are more Wicca 101 books out there than I could shake a stick at. And for that matter the majority of animal magic books I've seen look to be rather similar: massive encyclopedic compendiums that tell you about an animal, and the correspondences, but limit the ideas to how you can work with totem spirits. What is lacking are approaches that involve actually creating new techniques and approaches for doing animal magic, or, even more radically, coming up with a magical system focused entirely on animal magic.

So in February of 2005, when I met Lupa via Livejournal.com and she mentioned her book, I was intrigued. My first foray into magic was shamanism, mixed in with Hermeticism, but I'd never really done any totemic magic workings or any other animal magic workings beyond finding a familiar to work with. And though I'd looked through the occasional animal magic book, I just didn't find anything that really piqued a desire for me to do anything with what I found.

But a big advantage of being an editor for an occult publisher is that not only do I get to decide what books we'll publish and that I get to read those books before anyone else does (and, for that matter, to try out the ideas before anyone else), but I also get to learn more about magic and I get paid for it. Quite a bargain, if you ask me. And fortunately, when I told Lupa about Immanion Press, she was willing to consider getting her book published by a publisher that was only starting to make a name for itself in the occult scene.When I got her book and started to edit it, I was extremely pleased to find a book on animal magic that wasn't a carbon copy of every other animal magic book out there. Instead, I found a practical manual for working animal magic, ideas and experiments that could be readily implemented by any person who has some knowledge of occultism. I found a book that didn't fit into a niche, a book that had a unique approach and voice. I found this book.

The editing process for this book also saw generation of more ideas, and even of opportunities to work together. In fact, in some ways this book is responsible for bringing Lupa into my life, not just as one of my writers, but also as my mate. I can't guarantee it'll do the same for you, but I can say it will offer you fresh perspectives on animal magic, on what it is and how you can approach it. The real key to successful magic is not doing what other people have done, but rather cultivating an approach toward innovation and creativity that allows you to take what you learn from other people and gives you new perspectives on not only how you do magic, but how you live life and solve situations that occur in it.

You will know you are cultivating such perspectives when you can take a book like this and not only do the practices the author suggests, but are inspired to come up with your own approaches that meet the needs of your particular situations. In my case, I learned a lot from this book. It opened my eyes to new techniques for creating entities, as well as learning to establish a closer rapport with my familiar. It even gave me ideas on how I could work on the health of my own body by actively incorporating totem magic into my inner alchemical work.

Beyond that however, creativity and innovation is important for advancing our knowledge of the world around us. Instead of just repeating what other people have written, it's important to actually advance the knowledge in a given field you write in. By doing so, you are contributing to the continued validity of that field's existence, as well as giving rise to new opportunities, experiments, and research. This should be the aim of all writing done on magic. Sadly, the majority of the occult publishing industry is only focused on the "sure sale", 101 books written for beginners that do nothing for the advanced or intermediate magician. And yet even these teenagers find that the 101 books are not enough. We need books, ideas, approaches that go beyond the initial experience of magic. We need books that support an approach to experimentation in occult communities, and support the drive to go beyond what the established authors have written about.

This book is one of those books. This book advances magic into new directions. Of course, that's a bold claim for me to make. But you'll never know until you find out for yourself. Read the book. Work the exercises. Learn. Grow. Experiment.

May the magic you are finding bless your endeavors.

Taylor Ellwood
November 2005
Kent, OH

Introduction

Humans have long recognized the inherent qualities of nonhuman animals. Both on the physical plane and within the ethereal they symbolize desirable traits, lead through a Zen-like example of existence in the moment and offer guidance from a primitive world that has become increasingly separated from civilization through our own actions. By observing them and working with them in our practices we can tap into what they have to offer as well as provide them with the aid they need to survive in often-diminishing, ever-changing habitats.

Magicians, witches, shamans and their ilk have developed dozens of ways to work with animal energies. Physical animals in the wild act as avatars of archetypes while their tamed relatives enhance magical acts as familiars. Totemic bonds have been cultivated between animal spirits and humans for thousands of years. Controversially, the physical forms of animals at times become sacrifices to deities and other beings and are used for magical tools. The sheer multitude of rituals involving animals attests to the power we have discovered in them, and while the worst of these rites have involved great cruelty, the best exemplify the beauty and practicality of a working relationship between a magician and another living being.

Animal magic is accessible to any practicing magician. Many beginners are attracted to totemism and familiars for their portrayal in modern neopagan culture as purveyors of wisdom and internal strength. More advanced practitioners often seek animal magic as a way to find power in simplicity, to hone their own instincts or to add variety to their repertoire. Some dedicate their entire lives to working with familiars, while others seek a tertiary totem to aid with a single spell. Animal magic is incredibly versatile, as biodiversity ensures an animal energy for any need.

Some people appear to have some impressive natural abilities when it comes to animal magic. I've heard practitioners brag about how animals cluster around them whenever they meditate outside, follow them around when they're walking down the street, constantly show up in their everyday lives and dreams, *ad nauseam*. Methinks they're trying too hard to convince me–and themselves (of course, I could just be bitter because the bunnies and birds don't come to me in massive droves).

Seriously, though, you don't need to be Snow White in the forest with all the happy little wild creatures dancing around you as you sing pretty tunes (in fact, if you have wildlife walking up to you regardless of what you're singing you may want to suspect rabies on the part of the animal). I tend to get along pretty well with cats and dogs, even ones that are normally on the antisocial side. But that's due to years of experience and honing my body language and vocal tone, not because I believe I have some inherent critter charm about me. At most they

13

sense that I'm friendly, and I'm able to enhance that trust because of my ability to communicate in their language. Body language and tone of voice go a long way with domestic animals in particular. It is magic, but in a practical, common-sense manner rather than some wild "animal charmer" idea. If you're an animal telepath, more power to you. If not, don't let that fact discourage you. I've yet to have a single dog respond to a mental command in my years of working with the species.

You don't even need to share your home with a physical animal to be able to perform animal magic. Totem magic, for example, is quite easily done without a single cockroach in the cupboard. Having an animal familiar does require a pet of sorts, but many of the core concepts contained in that particular chapter may be applied to a magical construct or animal spirit guide as well as a physical animal; I simply concentrate on physical familiars due to the lack of material in regards to them.

I suppose you could do animal magic even if you loathe animals, but I would imagine that would create a strain on any relationship from the outset.

I wanted to avoid doing a rewrite of the books that are already out there. There are plenty of decent beginners' guides that contain dictionaries of animal symbolism and prefabricated spells and rituals based around animals in various forms. This book serves as a guide for the magical practitioner who creates hir own rituals, spells and sigils and who is capable of drawing hir own conclusions about the messages an animal spirit is

14

sending. There are a couple of my own creations in the appendices that you're welcome to use, but I wanted to avoid them becoming the focus of my writing.

This is a primal guide to animal magic – primal in two distinct manners. The first is that it is purely practical and bare-bones. I don't have a dictionary of animal totems. I don't include pages upon pages of pre-fabricated spells and formulae. Instead, I offer the tools necessary for building an individual practice of animal magic in its varying forms. I want the material to be able to mesh with a variety of paths rather than being a set system.

It is also primal in its ferocity. I don't pull punches. I tackle controversial topics like animal sacrifice and the use of animal parts in magic. I bring in obscure and experimental angles like cryptozoology and the art of inventing new species. In addition, I'm taking an amoral stance in this book. Amoral is not the same as immoral. Amoral means neither moral nor immoral–in short, I'm not going to make your moral decisions for you. I offer the information on neutral grounds and only in rare instances do I make any suggestions whatsoever where I feel they're necessary. It's up to you to make your own decisions and boundaries.

Blame my practice of Chaos and experimental magic. I'm a big fan of breaking boundaries and rethinking structures. This is a great resource for the syncretic practitioner who wants the basics on this paradigm, as well as for the more in-depth animal magic practitioner who's read everything else and wants to try my take on for size.

Finally, you may note my use of the words "hir" and s/he." American English has no concept of a personal gender-neutral pronoun; I use these additions to even things out. Feel free to steal them—they're hardly copyrighted.

I hope you enjoy what I offer and can reap much benefit from it. Keep in mind that all of this is from my own viewpoint and therefore subject to my own bias. I'm always open to feedback, good, bad or truly snarky. You can reach me at chaohippie@excite.com, through my website http://www.thegreenwolf.com or catch some blogging action on Livejournal—my username is lupabitch. I love to talk shop, too, so feel free to drop me a line!

Love,
Lupa

Chapter 1
Totemism

What are totems?

Totemism is probably the most widely-practiced form of animal magic today. Just about every magical practitioner has heard of it, and a significant portion work with them on a regular basis. At least once a week via message boards and forums I find some newbie asking "How do I find my totem?" Armed with a vague idea as to who and what these incorporeal entities are, the neophyte is eager to embark on a journey that goes well beyond having a favorite animal.

I have heard several theories as to what totems are, all, some or none of which may be true. These are some of the more common modern ideas of totems.

–Embodiment of an archetype: This stems from the concept of the Animal Master as described by Joseph Campbell: "He is a manifestation of that point, principle, or aspect of the realm of essence from which the creatures of his species spring" (Primitive Mythology — 1984/Campbell/p. 292). As per Campbell, a shaman petitioned this entity to release enough animals for food in exchange for certain rituals of respect or other offerings. The shaman also sometimes acted as a "lure" to draw prey animals over a cliff or into a trap. In this particular interpretation, what we know as totems today are in effect the result of evoking the Animal Masters of animal species. Individual animal spirit guides were also considered to be projections of a species' qualities rather than disembodied animal ghosts.

–Spirit guides: Some folks consider their personal totems to be more along the lines of individual animal spirits. Whether or not they've inhabited a physical body in the past seems to vary. Totemists who work along this path tend to form close, personal relationships with their totems, even to the point of either naming them or asking them what name they prefer.

–Psychological aspects: There are a few magicians who consider totems–and other spiritual entities–to be solely embodiments of internal aspects of the personality, much the same way that many paleopagan pantheons contain a complete spectrum of the human psyche in anthropomorphized form.

I personally am a big fan of a combination microcosm/macrocosm model. To wit, it serves me best to believe that when I call upon a totem I am both evoking an outer entity (I tend towards the archetypal theory) and invoking a certain portion of myself that corresponds to that entity. It strengthens the bond between me and that animal by helping me to remember that we are, by nature, interconnected. It also prevents me from becoming too psychological about the totem and passing it off as merely a figment of my imagination, thereby destroying some of the respect that I find comes with the territory on both ends. I've found that during times when I have erred too far in the direction of the microcosmic model the totems have a tendency to assert their reality upon my personal paradigm–not in harmful ways, mind you, simply actions that cause me to think twice about taking them for granted.

Paleopagan Totemism

The etymology of the word "totem" comes from the Ojibwe word *ototeman*, loosely "he is a relative of mine"(Totemism — 1962/*Levi-Strauss*/p. 18). This reflects the tendency in that particular culture for totemism to center around the family, clan or tribe, a trend that is similar in the majority of paleopagan totemic cultures. While the term totem comes from an American indigenous culture, the concept of totemism is found in cultures worldwide, both extinct and thriving.

Paleopagan totemism is primarily found in hunter/gatherer societies, and, to a more abstract degree, agricultural ones. "[T]wo attitudes towards the natural world and specifically towards mammals may be discerned: one, the sacramental egalitarian, associated with hunter-gatherers; the other, implying an ethic of opposition and control (rather than domination) associated with agriculturalists" (The Power of Animals — 1998/*Morris*/p. 4). While Morris was specifically referring to Malawi (Africa), this trend is global. Totemism arose in part as a response to human interaction with the natural world. The further from nature a culture is, the more divorced from its totemic ways it becomes. Hence we see strong totemic systems within indigenous African, American and Australian societies, totemism filtered into symbolic structures of religion in Greek and Roman societies and the heraldic system in medieval Europe.

Anthropologically speaking, totemism is very much a part of the social fabric of a culture structured around what amounts to one or more extended families in a relatively small group. It arose as a way not only to impress certain taboos on the individual society, but also as a means of separating or uniting people and of imparting certain knowledge to the younger generations.

Totemism was and is, among other things, a way to divide larger groups of people into more specific ones. Exogamy–marriage arranged according to one's clan or birthgroup–is aided and determined by the often matrilineal totemic system. In such systems, except in rare cases, people do not marry someone within their own totemic group; to do so breaks the taboo of incest. The clans are grouped under the auspices of animals each culture deems to be important and which are, for the most part, wild creatures. Exceptions do occur. For instance, in some groups of Ojibwe the Europe-derived pig and chicken became clan heads as a way to include members of the tribe of mixed indigenous and European blood (Totemism — 1962/*Levi-Strauss*/p. 21).

Clan-based totems are not necessarily venerated. Sometimes they are simply of the same importance as one's surname, as with the Ojibwe in Levi-Strauss's studies. Other times they gain a peculiar symbolism, as in the case of the masculine and feminine totems of some Australian aboriginal tribes. In these cultures certain animals are associated only with men or only with women. If a dispute arises between the sexes, one group sometimes kills a physical representative of the other's totem as a sign of protest or to incite a confrontation.

For some peoples the clan totem is either a symbolic or mythic progenitor of that particular group. In earlier times it was believed and/or known that humans and animals could trade forms fluidly and at will, and it wasn't until more recently that physical forms became more static. Therefore many animal characters in American indigenous mythologies often act out the tales in a human form, and it is considered by some perfectly reasonable for a family or clan to have been literally descended from an animal ancestor. This concept also existed within early Celtic beliefs, a cultural structure similar in its dependence on and reverence for the cycles and observable patterns of nature (The Life and Death of a Druid Prince —

1989/*Ross and Robins*/p. 59).

Spirit guides are a different story; in most groups the individual and group totems are seen as separate entities on unique systems (Totemism — 1962/*Levi-Strauss*/p. 18). While the clan totem is often seen as simply symbolic and embodying certain morals or marriage taboos, the individual guide is a more personal entity.

For some tribes, especially in parts of North America, the discovery of one's individual guide is a rite of passage. Upon reaching puberty, boys (and often, though, not always, girls) embark on a spiritual quest to ascertain whether they have a guardian animal spirit or not. Those who return in failure are often relegated to the lowest ranks of the tribe, while great ceremony greets those with more fortune. Often this is the time at which the person casts away hir old name and receives a new one, which may include the name of the guardian animal species.

Arthur C. Parker makes an intriguing comment on the guardian spirit quest: "As a psychological experience it seems to have been a reflection of all the religious beliefs and suggestions that had been absorbed" (The Indian How Book — 1975/*Parker*/p. 232). This suggests that the animal with which the seeker felt the most kinship is the one that embodies the qualities that the person, consciously or subconsciously, seeks to reproduce in hirself. And again, while the determination and expression of moral and social limits tends to be more the function of group-based totemism, Parker's theory suggests that the individual guide also serves to instruct the person it guards in proper behavior. Thus it is that animal archetypes and spirits are a very socially-oriented convention.

There are also cultures for whom the individual animal concept is again divided. Michael Harner references Carlos Castaneda's differentiation between the "tonal" and "nagual" animals. The former is determined by the time of birth and is similar to an astrological sign as well as the common concept of the clan animal (only, obviously, for the individual). The latter is the more specialized, actual animal spirit guide (The Way of the Shaman — 1990/*Harner*/p. 63).

The Quechua have a similar concept. They refer to the *nahual* animal, which is determined by day of birth. The relationship between the person and their *nahual* is very close, as if they are reflections of each other. In fact, the *nahual* may be used not only to explain a person's behavior, but to even excuse undesirable behavior. While that animal may be known to the parents of a child from birth, the child will not be told the animal's identity until s/he has reached maturity. Also of note is the idea that there may be more than one *nahual* animal per person, though all will be of the same species (The Family of Earth and Sky — 1994/*Elder and Wong*/p. 25-26).

For magic-workers the relationship is more specialized. This is found to be the case in many areas of southeast Australia, where the totemic bond between a "sorcerer" and the animal borders on what has often been described in classic European witchcraft as the animal familiar. "The animal lends it assistance to the sorcerer, on the one hand as a beneficent or maleficent agent, and on the other as a messenger or spy. Cases are known of the sorcerer exhibiting a tamed animal as proof of his power" (Totemism — 1962/*Levi-Strauss*/p. 37).

The relationship between the magician and hir animal guide or familiar is more specialized and intense than that of the everyday society member and hir own guardian spirit. Since the magician travels regularly into alternate realms and does battle with entities and other magic-workers, the animal spirit has much more work in protecting and aiding the human. S/he also communicates not only with hir own guardians, but also with those of hir patients; a common practice in many cultures is for hir to travel to the underworld to retrieve an ill person's personal animal, an act that will restore health.

The specific qualities attributed to totem animals, whether clan-based or individual, were initially drawn from close observation of the physical counterparts of each species. Cultures with totemic systems are invariably affected by the natural environment on a daily basis, and the interaction with animals is key to survival. Prey animals must be watched closely if they are to be successfully hunted or trapped, and predators can often teach humans hunting techniques through demonstration. More abstract concepts were extrapolated from the basic behaviors–large predators often morphed into symbols of warrior virtues, while wily animals became trickster characters in lore.

This observation wasn't always a passive thing. Joseph Epes Brown passed on the words of Brave Buffalo of the Oglala Lakhota: "Let a man decide upon his favorite animal and let him make a study of it...let him learn to understand its sounds and motions. The animals want to communicate with man, but *Wakan-Tanka* does not intend they shall do so directly–man must do the greater part in securing an understanding" (Animal of the Soul — 1997/*Brown*/p. 13).

Neopagan Totemism

Where traditional totemism is heavily group-oriented, with the individual animal guides often having less importance, the opposite is true of neopagan totemism. A lot of this stems from a lack of culture. By that I don't mean that neopagans are a mass of rude slobs (though some would heartily say otherwise!). Rather, for the most part neopagans come from mega-cultures in which the social ties are much weaker than in smaller tribes and family groups. Take American culture, for example. The nuclear family is stronger than the extended family for many people, and yet compared to the family ties of indigenous cultures these family units are incredibly loose. Today it isn't uncommon for a person to have relatives scattered across an entire country, or even over several continents. Needless to say there isn't much room for traditional lore to be passed on amid the empty chatter of the various technological media that dominate our communication today; religion tends to be prepackaged, and family history is relegated to the halls of genealogy.

Since few neopagans and magicians are raised within a magical tradition, and a proportionately small number become involved in working or teaching groups on a long-term basis, again there is a lack of emphasis on group work. The number of solitaries most decidedly is larger than the number of practitioners in formal groups.

As a result, when neopagans study totemism it is primarily with the individual practitioner in mind. The concepts of the tribal or family totem and the individual animal guide have become blended into one idea that is a result of adaptation to changes in social structure.

Neopagans draw happily from a number of cultural wells when it comes to totems, combining elements of both traditional group and individual totemism. While most of the source material–such as it is–is at least somewhat based on assorted Native American lore, there have also been attempts to recreate Celtic totemism, and the occasional bold soul will even delve into Australian totemic beliefs. Unfortunately, given the high rate of cultural appropriation, a lot of information is suspect; some neopagans and New Agers will often talk about "Native American totemism" without respect to specific tribes, and very few venture into other cultures for information. This is why I have tended to look more towards anthropological texts in regards to paleopagan totemism rather than relying on neopagan information, with only a few exceptions.

In addition, trying to find legitimate written information on modern paleopagan totemism, if you aren't born into it, is rather difficult. A sizable proportion of the books on what is presented as authentic Native American spirituality is penned by what have become termed "plastic shamans", people who exploit tribal spirituality for personal gain. (If you really wanted to, you could include me in that category, given that I'm a European mutt with absolutely no official tribal training of any sort, and I'm talking about totemism, using an Ojibwe-derived term. However, I've never presented myself as anything other than European mutt, with no authority beyond my own personal experience. It's also one of the reasons my name is Lupa, and not Running-Wolf-in-Trees or something equally contrived.)

Globalism may have negatively affected totemism, but it has also been beneficial. Because we are more aware of the diversity of species, the animal energies not native to our home are able to communicate with us without getting a resounding "Huh???!!!" in response. A couple of hundred years ago if, say, Gazelle tried talking to an Inuit shaman, the message wouldn't be as easily received as from Caribou. These days since we're more receptive to non-native animals (and know what they are)

29

it's easier for them to contact us if they're what's most appropriate. Even if we've never seen or heard of the animal we can still learn quite a bit from reading about them, watching documentaries of them, and, if possible, seeing them at a zoo or wildlife park. And there's also more information to be had by contacting the totem hirself and finding out that species' unique spiritual traits. In addition, many practitioners blaze their own trails and create their own traditions as they go along when working with these animal entities.

There are folks who claim to have fantastic animals such as unicorns, gryphons and the ever-popular dragons as totems. It varies from person to person whether or not this is considered "true" totemism. On the one hand, totems teach people how to interact with this physical, solid world, and an animal that is not native to this place may very well have difficulty in doing so. There's also the camp that argues that these animals don't even really exist, so how can they teach anyone anything at all? On the other hand, a few folks, particularly within the Otherkin community, surmise that perhaps at one point we did have physical dragons and other such creatures on this plane. If this is so (and I make no decision either way) then it's been so long ago that the world has had time to sufficiently change to the point that their knowledge may be alien to us. The same goes for long-extinct species like dinosaurs. After a point the world may have sufficiently changed so that the information is less relevant

On the other hand, if the definition of totemism is expanded a bit, fantastic and extinct animals are perfectly capable of filling the same role in our lives as traditional totems. Totems teach us lessons about existence in general, and while animals that do not physically coexist with us may not always fully understand our place in space and time, this does not negate the lessons they do have to teach. And, to an extent, the balance of species in natural habitat has remained more or less the same no matter what permutations Nature has gone through. The animals may change, but the niches are more or less the same.

The number of totems a person possesses (if one may use such a term) varies widely according to whom you're asking. Some folks insist that each person is allotted one totem in a lifetime. Others work with a dualistic model, often along male/female or masculine/feminine lines with a corresponding left/right side association. Beyond that I've heard four (one for each cardinal direction), five (add in the center), six (cardinal directions + up and down), seven (add the center again) and even beyond that.

There is also an offshoot of psychotherapy that involves animal symbolism and the seven primary chakras. The Personal Totem Pole, developed by Eligio Stephen Gallegos in the early 1980's, allows the patient to identify the animal s/he associates with each individual chakra. The therapist then guides the patient in communicating with these animals as the patient and the creatures all develop. It's definitely worth looking into for anyone who works with either totemism or chakras. While designed for use in the therapist's office, the techniques discussed can be easily adapted to individual needs by the experienced magician. I don't recommend that newcomers do quite such heavy tinkering with their psyches until they've had some prior experience with a book designed for unguided self-help, such as Robert Anton Wilson's *Prometheus Rising.*

I've had much success working with the Personal Totem Pole model. My first self-guided meditation yielded very clear visions of the animals associated with my chakras–not only what animals they were, but their state of health and what I needed to do to help them, and thereby myself. Since then I have been able to communicate with each animal to continue my growth and healing processes, a rewarding experiment in and of itself. I highly recommend Gallegos' works for anyone interested in using totemic magic for personal metamorphic purposes. For more information on the chakras themselves try *Wheels of Life* by Anodea Judith.

Through a guided meditation, similar to the one found in Appendix A, I introduced myself to the animals located at each of my seven primary chakras. The root was a snake; heavy and bloated with black bile, sluggish and sad. The stomach contained a fox swimming in the black bile; it was from that part of me that the vile stuff like oozing tar originated. My solar plexus was a strong bay horse, full of energy, but unable to do

32

anything more than rear in place, frustrated and angry.

My heart, the primary source of my issues, was a very timid, flighty wolf who ran when approached. The throat contained a loud, snarling leopard. My third eye was a large purple dragon with an impressive hoard and a stone egg that he clutched quite tightly. At the crown was a regal white hermaphroditic deer with antlers, aloof and distant.

In working with these animals I began to figure out some of the root causes for issues I'd been working with for years. The snake was bloated because she was trying to keep the bile in my stomach from spreading to the rest of my body by absorbing it into herself. This directly correlated to my own stomach issues; years of stress and poor dietary habits had turned that organ into an acidic mess. The physical problems translated into the black bile that, energetically, often covered my entire body. A trip to the doctor's office and some bloodwork confirmed that I was also hypoglycemic–if my blood sugar dropped because I wasn't eating enough my mood plummeted, my stress level shot up and the stomach acid increased, putting more pressure on my system as a whole. As I improved my diet and began to relax more the amount of this bile reduced dramatically. My snake became less bloated and more active, and my fox was finally able to start cleaning herself up. It was also at this point that Fox as a secondary totem came into my life and took over the primary position for a time, allowing Wolf to take a break.

Poor Wolf. My heart chakra was such a mess. She'd been caring for me for years, but was so scared of everything that her nerves were shot. She was constantly nipping at Horse's heels, wondering why he didn't move. She always cried to Leopard, who snarled at the world in an attempt to protect her. And she added to the stress in general, causing the poor Fox to be flooded with even more bile. Allowing Wolf to take a much-needed vacation let every other animal relax. Horse intimated to me that he would be best as a focus in my personal work, rather than the frustrations of a day-to-day job, so I began to use his energy more for my creative pursuits. Leopard's main concern was protecting Wolf; he was always concerned for her health. He simply wanted her to stop crying and didn't know what to do besides attack whatever had caused her to cry. When she settled down, he was able to breathe more and snarl less, looking at the situation without speaking first.

Dragon and Stag were more mysterious; they essentially said that they wouldn't participate until the other five animals were healthier. As of this writing they're still relatively silent, observing in their own ways.

The one who's really come to the fore has been Fox. As you'll read in a minute, she became my secondary totem in the summer of 2005. Since then she's been a very strong influence in my life, doing everything from improving my sense of humor and reminding me to confront the various annoyances and ills of my life with laughter to increasing my awareness of magic.

These lessons have improved even my physical life–my stomach issues began to lessen once she began her work.

My work with the Personal Totem Pole model is a bit different from the other totemic model I will discuss momentarily. The former, for my purposes, is primarily a symbolic model. The animals therein are purely internal, and the characteristics they carry correlate directly to the state of the chakras they represent. My actual totems are a microcosmic/macrocosmic model as described earlier, and their traits stem from a combination of the archetypal energies and my own connections to them. While some of the shifts in my chakra totems mirrored that of my other totems, I consider them to be different entities.

Through my own experiences and studies I have in addition developed a unique system for categorizing and working with totem animals, based on specific characteristics of the bond between the totem and the practitioner. I divide them into three categories: primary, secondary and tertiary. This is the model I will be working with throughout this chapter, but the concepts can be applied to any neopagan totemic system.

–Primary totems: These are the totems that are with you for the majority of your life. They are the animal(s) whose characteristics pervade everyday life, and who spend a lifetime teaching fundamental lessons about the Self and interaction with the world. One is common, and two to three is not unheard of, but more than that is exceedingly rare. Some people internalize their primary totem to the point of a therianthropic bond (see Chapter 5 for more information). While occasional incidents of primary totems changing in a lifetime do occur, generally these animals are permanent teachers.

–Secondary totems: When you have a specific lesson you need to learn or a certain quality that must be nurtured, secondary totems will arrive in your life of their own volition specifically for that purpose. They generally announce their presence by increasing their presence in your life until you take notice. Once you have picked up whatever it is they've brought you they take their leave of you. How long they stay varies greatly according to what needs to be done and how stubborn you are in cooperating. There doesn't seem to be any set number of these in a lifetime, though usually no more than two or three will show up at once unless you're doing some major metamorphic magic, magic that is used to affect change within one's own self. . The appearance of a secondary totem means that the practitioner must focus on a specific part of hir life. The number of secondaries must necessarily be limited, or no progress will be made.

– Tertiary: Contrary to some neopagan literature, you can ask totems to come into your life for help with specific magic. It's not the same as the often-belittled "choosing your totem;" rather, it is simple evocation. Nothing more is required than that you decide which totem(s) will be able to help you with your need, form whatever relationship you see fit, and then proceed to work together to make the magic happen. Again, there's no limit on how many tertiary totems you can work with, and the relatively brief lifespan of the bond seems to be the primary limiting factor here.

These are generalized categories. There are instances of overlapping totemic roles. For instance, in the middle of writing this book I experienced a changing of the guard, so to speak. Wolf, my primary, had been exhibiting heightened weaknesses in the form of nervousness and extreme reactions to normal displays of dominance and submission in my interactions with other people. She'd always been the main totemic influence in my life, for better or for worse, and any attempt to allow another energy in for balance was met with a flash of fangs and a snarl. At one point I (and she) became overwhelmed by the stress and pressure of imbalanced traits; it took a few harmful and embarrassing experiences, a powerful pathworking and an elemental influence to finally make her realize that she needed to back off. It was about time, too–she was exceptionally frayed and tired.

Enter Fox. Fox was gentle, feminine (though not necessarily female) and sensual, and a consummate magician.

He smoothed out the intensity of Wolf, softened the hard, defensive edges and revitalized burned-out areas of my psyche with her gentle energy. His sense of humor reminded us both to laugh more, and his taking over of the primary position allowed Wolf to take a much-needed rest.

During this period Wolf was still my primary totem, in that she had the most influence on my behavior overall. Identifying as Fox for a period, however, allowed me to make necessary changes to myself that Wolf couldn't provide. Secondary totems, many times, do enter into our lives in order to balance out the flaws and weaknesses of our primary totem(s). Occasionally they remain and become essentially primary totems themselves, having as much influence over us as their predecessors. Once the balance is struck, both the old and new totems often work together to create a more harmonious internal environment. So far, Fox has remained a strong presence in my life and continually comes up with new lessons for me to learn. Even when Wolf returned to the primary role she originally occupied, Fox was given a place of high priority in my life.

This process of change occurred even before I realized what had happened. Wolf took her first vacation from guiding me when I was a teenager. Somewhere around the age of eleven, I got the stereotypical fascination with horses that a lot of girls that age go through. I learned to draw them and that was the vehicle through which that particular totem entered my life. Horse took over the primary role in my life. Equine behaviors overshadowed lupine ones and the subconscious magic I created was from the prey's point of view rather than the predator's. Horse helped me get through my teen years, an awkward, coltish time. He reminded me to not pay too much attention to the dominance and submission displays that are so exaggerated in the junior and senior high school arenas (and in wolf packs), but instead to pay attention to my own herd and the rapid growth I was experiencing on many levels at the time. He stayed with me until my realization of magic at the age of seventeen, then chose to relinquish her position to Wolf again.

The difference between Wolf, and Fox and Horse, is that I always go back to Wolf, who never entirely leaves. Horse stayed long enough to get me through a specific period of my life, then returned me to Wolf's care. Fox, as I've stated, is still aiding me in my path. Again, keep in mind that I'm using general categories, and that individuals may find some differences in their own personal systems.

Occasionally there is tension between paleopagan and neopagan totemists. In any field of study there will always be those who are neophobic and believe that anyone who deviates from specific patterns is not only disrespecting but also diluting the effectiveness and "truth" of said field. While I agree that a lot of indigenous culture has been appropriated, changed on a whim and taken way out of context, totemism is something that is essentially universal. All human societies have totemic

39

traditions either surviving in pockets or left over in legend and lore. The way we view the natural world has affected how we interact with totems. I have spent the years since I started practicing in 1998 with a complete lack of any tradition to teach me proper methods of totemic magic and can still boast a decent success rate. In other words–if it works, use it. If working within a strict Lakhota paradigm is what you feel you need, go with it. If you're an unapologetic buffet-style Chaote, feel free to work with whomever you need to get the job done. The rest of this chapter deals with neopagan totemism, which is a lot more flexible than most paleopagan traditions, and so the prerequisites are a lot less strict. Magic overall is an incredibly personal thing and the only one who can determine what works for you, is you.

The Search Begins

The first thing the average beginner wants to know about totems is never "what is a totem," but "how do I find MY totem?" This should be undertaken after you have a basic understanding of who and what totem animals are, if for no other reason than it gives you a context within which to work. This doesn't necessarily mean immersing yourself in a paleopagan culture; rather, have an idea of just what sort of magic you'll be getting yourself into. A reading of a book or three from the bibliography and suggested reading list will help, but isn't absolutely necessary. Much can be learned from practice alone, and totems tend to be quite forgiving of neophytes.

The most common method of totem identification is the guided meditation. This can either be performed solo or with a mentor. The basic formula is: enter into a relaxed state, visualize a setting into which your totem can arrive, see and communicate with your totem, come back up for air. Pretty much all variations follow those steps. You can find my example in Appendix A of this book, or create one of your own.

Totem-based divination cards have become incredibly popular in the past decade. While some wince at the cultural appropriation some of these decks' creators — and users — practice, the cards themselves are as effective as any other tool of divination. The key to success is in the diviner, not the tool. Most of these involve several dozen cards, each with a different animal on it. Generally the reading involves selecting a certain number of cards that will reveal the querent's totems. While I'm not a big fan of using cards for primary totems, I do use a particular deck for finding suggested tertiary totems. Keep in mind that these decks severely limit the possible choices, usually only including a standard set of mammals, a few birds and other animals.

My personal choice is the *Animal-Wise Tarot* deck from Ted Andrews. This deck and I worked out an original, elemental/directional reading format that works wonders for tertiary totem readings. As with any tarot deck, this one is divided into the Major Arcana and the four suits of the Minor Arcana. I divided the deck into five sub-decks—one for the Major and one for each of the Minor. The Major Arcana sat in the center of the reading and represented Spirit, the center of one's being. The suit of Pentacles/Earth I placed in the North, Wands/Air in the East, Swords/Fire in the South, and Cups/Water in the West. When giving a reading I have the querent shuffle each sub-deck separately and draw one card from each. The North details the querent's mundane life—home, work, family, money. The East deals with the intellect, with things such as teaching, learning and planning. The West works with emotions and the influences on them, and often is tied closely to the East. The Center is the core of Being, the reserve of energy that the querent should call upon when all else fails. South is change and the method by which one should perform active change in hir life. The animal in each of these positions is the one to call upon when working with that area of life.

In some cases, the totem's identity is information that is simply, intuitively, known. I've been a Wolf's child since I was a toddler. My family has always owned German Shepherds, and at the time we had a large black dog who tended to hang out on the patio just outside the back door. One day I saw him standing out there, looking into the woods at the back of the yard. He didn't look quite like himself, as I recall, and my thought at the time was, "Wow, he looks just like a wolf!" For some reason, that allowed Wolf to make a connection with me that never faded. After that, Wolf and wolves became a strong part of my personality.

There is much debate as to whether a lifelong fascination with an animal gives it totem status or not. On the one hand a strong attraction to a certain species can be a marker of a totemic bond, especially if it occurs at a young age. On the other, such an early focus can create a self-fulfilling prophecy, and the seeker may consciously or unconsciously adopt behaviors of the animal in everyday life. This doesn't necessarily mean that it isn't a totemic bond; I for one believe that the creation of that bond doesn't have to be wholly passive on the part of the person. By this I mean that the human may just as easily extend a hand towards the primary totem as the totem can spark the growth with a paw, hoof or wing. The difference between this situation and a secondary totemic relationship is that the latter is more short-term. Also, the key trait of a totemic bond is the increase in adopted behavior of the animal on the part of the human.

Obsessions with the primary totem can create a barrier to making a connection with secondary totems. For example, for the longest time I was incredibly lupo-centric about things. While Wolf gave me a lot, I kept ignoring the contributions made by Horse, Cat and others. I was worried that working with them extensively would make me "less wolf." It wasn't until

I read an article by R.J. Stewart in *PanGaia* magazine that I was prompted to really evaluate the balance of the totems in my life. In this article, Stewart described a conversation he had with a Lakhota elder. At one point he had stated, "[T]he [totems] that choose you, even if you dislike them, are the most powerful for you, no matter what you think you want" (Ambassadors to the Animals — 2005/Stewart/p. 19). At the time I'd been reevaluating my past relationships with my own secondaries as they related to my primary, Wolf. For instance, I had come to resent Horse's presence in my life because he'd arrived at a time when I was very socially awkward–an outcast in high school–and so I began to blame him for being a bad influence. It was only after taking Stewart's comment into account that I began to see that Horse had been doing his best to help me through a very bad situation. He was there for me during the times when I wished so badly to be accepted that I almost gave in and tried to be just like everyone else, a practice that had failed miserably every time. Instead, he counseled me to be myself, to enjoy the freedom I had in my individuality amid my own herd and to take that freedom and run with it. It finally dawned on me that the totem I had thought was a curse was nothing of the kind.

I realized that secondaries can be just as powerful in their influence as primaries, and that pushing them away only stunts my growth. Sure, Wolf is still a strong part of me, but he works in tandem with Horse, Cat, Fox and several others, and it was only my stubbornness holding the partnership back. Totems are fluid beings, and even a primary totem can shift during a lifetime. Although a primary totem remains within a person's life for their entire span in this world, they do not always have the primary influence on that person. Horse and Fox have both acted in the primary position even though they were later arrivals in my life; this was due in part or a need at each time for a balance against Wolf's energies, which could be very intense. As stated previously, the primary/secondary/tertiary divisions are generalized and are merely my own way of understanding the varying roles totems have in my life.

Another common problem is the desire to have a more showy totem when the actual animal you need to speak to may not be so glamorous. Of course, I'm one to talk as one of seemingly jillions of Wolf totem people; however, there are plenty of cases of folks who have willfully ignored Rabbit or Frog while seeking out Bear or Tiger instead. Eventually these people find that the energies of the bigger animals work against them, and they find solace in the more humble teachers whose lessons empower them more than any great predator could. Either that, or they continue in their delusions until they ultimately become frustrated and give up entirely. There are theories as to why certain species do make more common bonds with humans in both totemic and therianthropic relationships. Wolves, for one, are thought by some to have passed on their social structure to early humans through example, and most certainly influenced our ancestors' hunting skills not only through their observation, but their practices of domestication. Still, even rare and obscure species have behaviors that we can learn from, so don't be turned off if you get frequent Kinkajou visits instead of the Bear you were hoping for.

Jessica Dawn Palmer, in her excellent work, *Animal Wisdom*, makes a point that's right on target in regards to less glamorous animals: "The bovine was as important in the Old World as the buffalo was to the Plains people of America" (Animal Wisdom — 2004/*Palmer*/p. 72). Considering that many of the American indigenous cultures on the Great Plains centered around the bison, it's easily understandable that the cow was an incredibly important animal in her own territory. In fact, you can still see the reverence for cattle in India, where cows roam the streets freely.

Also, don't discount an animal that is not of your country of origin. Early totemism was limited, of course, to animals in the environment the culture in question lived in. Now that we are in a much more global society we are able to better connect with animals we may never have seen in person. Thus it is perfectly acceptable for someone of Asian descent to have a coyote totem, or for someone whose roots are Celtic to work with Giraffe.

I'm not a big fan of omens, such as having a certain animal show up repeatedly either in the flesh or in symbols, because we have a tendency to anticipate and focus specifically on that animal to the exclusion of others. I noted this phenomenon in a different context. Up until 2001 I lived in Missouri, at which point I moved to Pennsylvania. It seemed to me that I always saw more Missouri plates than other out-of-state plates on the PA roads–until a friend of mine from upstate New York mentioned that he thought he saw more cars from that state than any other tooling around Pittsburgh. All too often we start looking for signs of a certain animal to the exclusion of all others–a tunnel vision which Robert Anton Wilson sums up as "Whatever the Thinker thinks, the Prover proves" (Prometheus Rising — 1983/*Wilson*/p. 3). Sure, it's neat when you see that red-tailed hawk every morning on the way to work, but let's keep Occam's Razor in our toolkit, shall we? If frequent sightings of an animal were a sole sign of a totem's arrival, everyone in downtown Pittsburgh would be learning at the foot of Pigeon.

Some people will assume that any animal sighting, if not a sign of a totem, is still always significant. I actually ran a bit of a magical experiment with counting crows for divination. When I first started reading meters in the more rural areas I started seeing a lot of crows. So I began using the following rhyme to divine with them:

"One's sorrow, two's mirth,
Three's a wedding, four's a birth
Five's a christening, six a death,
Seven's heaven, eight is hell,
And nine's the Devil his own self."

I would take whatever crows I saw as an omen towards whatever I was thinking of at the time I saw them, since my mind is almost always active. But after a while, I began to notice that a lot of the time the crows were wrong about whatever I was thinking about. I also found that many times I'd see, say, a single crow, and then 20 seconds later three crows. And then nothing would happen that was connected to either sighting. In the long run, I found no real correlation between crow sightings and any significant changes in my life. I suppose I could have, if I wanted to make every single tiny occurrence in my life that important—but after a while, divination taken too far becomes self-fulfilling prophecy, and rather than panicking over seeing a single crow and worrying over what disaster would befall me I decided to simply let the crows be crows.

Keep in mind, too, that a lot of animals are territorial, and that having a certain species appear suddenly in your life may just mean that a mated pair has decided to claim territory that happens to include your area. In addition, a lot of species, mostly birds, are migratory, and seeing a nonlocal species all of a sudden may simply mean that those animals are on their usual seasonal trip from one locale to another.

Animal visitors in dreams are also often assumed to be portentous. Before you make the totem assumption, though, take a moment to figure out what that animal means to you as an individual. Don't pick up one of those rather useless dream dictionaries that assume everyone's subconscious imagery is the same; instead, write down all the associations you place with that animal, and consider how you normally react to it. It may very well just be a symbol tossed up by your subconscious to represent a current issue or person in your life. Only you know what a particular animal means to you.

For further clarification, try divination. A simple yes/no format, such as a pendulum or coin toss, works quite nicely. Multiple queries—such as "best two out of three"—help make up for the natural margin of error. You can find out more information about this in Appendix B.

Don't be discouraged if you don't get immediate results. You may not be using the best method for you in your search, or the conditions in which you tried searching may not have been optimum. For instance, one of my early forays into the Otherworld was attempted about two hours after I got home from a rough day at work. Each time I tried to release myself and travel down into the tunnel I used, images from that day at work would shatter my visualization. Needless to say it was an aborted journey.

Also, the totem you seek may not feel ready to work

with you for some reason. This is a two-way deal, not just you drawing on another's energy, and totems have as much personality as you do. The totem may not feel you are ready, or may not feel up to the task hirself, or may just not want to work with you at all. If you get repeated failures with the same totem, perform a simple divination to determine why it's not working, then take some time off from the effort.

For some people totems may just not be the group of entities best suited for their magic. If you consistently have trouble getting results with totems, perhaps you're better off working with a different set of entities. Some people simply don't have a primary totem. There's nothing wrong with that, and this is why there are myriad magical paradigms to work within; the key is to find the ones that work best for you.

So I've Found My Totem. Now What?

There are numerous books out there that contain dictionaries of totemic symbolism. This is not one of those books. There are several I suggest, though, in the bibliography and other recommended reading. Don't rely solely on neopagan sources. The focus tends to be relatively narrow and occasionally the research is beyond shaky–it's flat-out wrong. Hence the unnamed popular pagan author who, confused about species differentiation and picking out-of-date resources, described the domestic ferret as having a brown summer coat and a white winter coat and possessing a thirst for blood–things that any responsible ferret owner will tell you are way out in left field.

Studying the behavior and habits of the physical counterpart to a totem is one of the most effective methods of learning from it. Many of the traditional totemic correspondences most likely stemmed from human observation of animal behavior. Bears, for instance, were observed by a number of cultures browsing for roots and plants. Some people came to the conclusion that as bears had a good knowledge of these plants, consequently Bear must have the quality of herbal knowledge as well. As herbs are sources of medicine even today, it wasn't a far leap to start communicating with Bear on healing issues. In addition, many humans associated bears very strongly with our own species, and anthropomorphized the behavior, assigning human qualities to the bears' actions. Other traits came about in a more direct manner; the female bear's famously vigilant maternal behavior is a wellspring of strength for parents.

Behavior is the strongest link we can study; after all, totems teach us about our own actions and habits. I've seen some references to less connected traits of the physical animals. I don't particularly believe that you should necessarily change your diet just because your totem eats something specific or change jobs so that you're more active when your totem is. Keep your personal human biology in mind, in particular preferred sleep patterns, food and other allergies and other physical limitations. I'd hate to think I'd convinced someone with a Cougar totem to drop out of a tree onto the back of a deer, attempt to break hir neck and instead have hir own neck broken! Less drastically, humans are biologically diurnal and omnivorous, and while some are able to adjust to a nocturnal schedule or vegetarian or vegan diet, make sure your body is capable of handling such changes. Don't assume that your totemic bond alone is capable of shifting your internal chemistry.

Things such as food and time of day, however, are excellent tools in magic. Make offerings of your totem's preferred diet in return for aid in magic (don't give the food to actual wildlife, though—more on that later in the chapter). Perform rituals with your totem when the physical animal is at its peak. Work your rituals in areas where the physical animal may be more common, if possible.

If your totem is domesticated be sure to research hir wild counterparts. Dogs are basically immature wolves because of the process by which we domesticated them—while there are a few that will constantly challenge us, they are never as dominant as a wild wolf is, and most of the instincts, except those which benefit us, are dampened or even removed. Keep this in mind when doing parallel research—Wolf is not the same as Dog, but Wolf can often help balance out Dog's weaknesses. Conversely, animals that may seem to be nearly identical aren't so similar. Bobcat and Lynx, while being similar in appearance, do possess unique personalities, and also inhabit some differing and some overlapping environs. Keep this in mind as you research.

Myths, legends and medieval bestiaries are more fodder for symbolism and magical inspiration, but again take them in context, especially the bestiaries. Medieval naturalists had some incredibly active imaginations, and some of the qualities they assigned to perfectly mundane animals are impossible even for humans today. Myths and legends often are several times removed from reality. Look at the demonization of the grey wolf. Despite years of thorough research made available to the public many people still think of that shy creature as a bloodthirsty marauder ready to slaughter any human in hir path.

When it comes to fantastic totems, myths and legends are about all we have to go on. In that case look to possible sources for those myths. Ancient stories of dragons are quite possibly inspired by the early discoveries of dinosaur bones, while everything from the ibex to the ox have been postulated as sources of unicorn mythos. This doesn't mean that these animals don't exist on some other plane of existence, but the physical animals that inspired stories of them ought to be studied to flesh out the information available, , along with evoking the fantastic totems themselves. As for extinct animals, contact with the totem is recommended to fill in the blanks where paleontology leaves off.

In fact, the most direct and thorough method of

discerning the teachings offered is by conversation with your totem. Repeatedly using the initial guided meditation in Appendix A is a good way to get into contact with the animal; in addition, it creates a more solid magical setting for you both to work within. With enough effort and energy expended into that setting entire rituals can be performed there without having to perform any ritual activity on the physical plane. Sometimes you'll find that a totem has lessons for you not mentioned in any book or set of lore. For instance, Deer has always been the Dreamkeeper for me, a role not extant in any mythos known to me. The closest correspondence I can find is of the white deer that, when hunted, leads the pursuers into a quest.

Divinatory tools may also be used in speaking with a totem. Again, yes/no methods may be used, or a more complex tool such as tarot, automatic writing or the dreaded ouija board can be implemented (A note on ouija boards and their cleaned-up cousins, angel and spirit boards: they are just tools. Nothing more. Remember that tarot cards once held the same negative stigma, and we've managed to dispel that stupidity pretty well. Anyone who ever had a bad experience with a ouija board was probably subconsciously expecting it).

Just keep in mind that each totem carries a unique message for each seeker. What Wolf tells me is not necessarily what Wolf tells you, nor may it be what Wolf tells another author. Books are good for sparking thought processes, but in the end the conversation between you and the totem is the most important message conveyed. Some hardcore totemists work exclusively with firsthand information.

Preconceptions about a totem can color the information you receive. There's much talk about the power of the Alpha wolf in the pack, no doubt a symptom of the macho bullshit that gets woven about any large predator by mainstream American society. My Wolf side used to be very Omega. When in a Wolfish mindset I tended to back down from confrontation of any sort. This is part of why, at one point, Cougar came into my life to teach me assertion. And, while we're on the subject of lupine stereotypes, you can just forget the "lone wolf" mystique. A lone wolf is almost invariably a doomed wolf in the wild, as the pack is necessary to bring down large game that is vital for winter survival. While a pack may temporarily disband when small game is prolific, it comes back together for times when group hunts are necessary or when young must be raised. Wolves are highly social creatures, and our misconceptions should not skew our acceptance of that reality and animal behaviors in general.

Strengthening the Bond

Once you have an idea of what lessons your totem has laid out for you, you need to start working with the totem not only to deepen your understanding of these lessons, but to put them into effect in your life. On a purely psychological level the following activities serve to create a stronger imprint of that animal in your mind, while on a magical level they communicate respect to your totem and increase the bond between you.

Creating a small shrine or altar to the totem is relatively simple. Set aside an area of your home–perhaps a shelf, wall or windowsill–and reserve it for that totem. Statues, pictures (including ones you create yourself), feathers, books, poems and other items pertaining to the totem may be placed in this space. A candle dedicated the animal can be burned at intervals for meditative or magical purposes.

You can also make periodic offerings at this shrine, including thank-you gifts after a successful magical collaboration. Foods that the animal's physical counterpart likes, small stones and trinkets, a specially charged candle, a piece of artwork or writing in the totem's honor are all good offerings. Many totems also appreciate either donations or volunteer time given to efforts to preserve the physical animals–Appendix D includes contact information for a number of organizations that focus on aiding domestic or wild animals.

A note on food offerings: contrary to what many believe, feeding wildlife is a bad idea. The increase in availability of food has led to more intrusion of wildlife in suburban and even blatantly urban areas. Whitetail deer and Canada geese are two of the more benign examples; however, in certain areas predators such as bears and mountain lions have been sighted near human city edges, and a number of metro areas have a marked problem with coyotes. While we magical folk may find these animals to be charming and even sacred, in reality their wanderings into our "territory" have nothing but negative side effects for them. When wildlife comes into contact with automobiles, household pets, garbage cans, or children the result is almost invariably bad for the animal. Furthermore, feeding wildlife can create dependency; after enough time, if the human food source is taken away, animals may starve because they're not used to finding food naturally. Save the food for indoor offerings, ritual meals or (reasonable) gifts to your pets. Better yet, donate commercial pet food to a local stray or wildlife shelter.

On a more esoteric level, the relationship between you and your totem can be developed through evocation and invocation. This includes both working and celebratory rituals. Evoke the animal not only when you need its guidance and energy for a magical purpose, but also any time you work magic; treat it as an honored guest along with all your other regular attendees. A totem at a Wiccan Sabbat, for instance, adds a certain wild energy to the turning of the Wheel. You may have a certain candle you light upon the evocation of your totem or a small figurine that represents it. Or you may have a specific bit of poetry or prose you recite any time you invite the totem into the working area. Not only will the totem enhance your magical efficacy, but it will appreciate the consideration, and you'll find yourself more adept at working with its energies as time goes on.

Invocation of a totem often falls under the area of nonphysical shapeshifting (more on that topic in Chapter 5). This involves calling the totem into yourself, allowing your ego to slide to the side and letting the totem take control to a certain extent. In effect you are embodying that energy and allowing it to work through your flesh. Some practitioners have a certain costume or set of ritual tools that they wear only for the invocation; others may utilize a part of the physical animal itself (see Chapter 6 for details). All these things serve as links to the totem itself to allow an easier mental shift. Invocation may be done in a number of ways; reciting a declaration of one's intent from the viewpoint of the totem, performing a dance otherwise mimicking the animal's movements or visualizing the totem entering your body are just a few suggestions.

For instance, one of the strongest acts of magic I've performed is dancing in a wolf skin at drum circles. It's an amazing experience; I feel the skin wrap around my like it's my own, and I can feel the spirit of the wolf that remains within the skin peering through my own eyes as he speaks to me of what it was like to be him. This hasn't just been a powerful influence on me; observers have reported everything from breaking down in tears of wonder to seeing me meld with the wolf spirit until reality blurred and it wasn't quite clear where my skin ended and the pelt began.

Obviously you don't need to wear a pelt–or any other animal part–to be able to utilize dance and other trances in honoring your totem. I've done dances without the pelt as well, and the effect is the same. It simply involves Wolf on a purely spiritual level without the added help of the spirit of the pelt.

It can be a difficult task to allow another entity to work through you, but be persistent–with practice you'll be able to allow yourself to make room for another. Just be sure to have a ready method of banishment in case you need to force the guest out–while totem animals are generally benign, exceptions occur. In addition you may find it difficult, especially early on in your practice, to shake the "high" of a solid invocation; be prepared to remove that energy from your system and reground yourself. You can perform a formal rite, such as the Lesser Banishing Ritual of the Pentagram (easily found online or in many ceremonial texts) or simply make up your own words to say farewell to the spirit. Make sure you eat and drink once you've cooled down so your body is well-cared-for and you don't contribute to the high with that spacey feeling malnourishment and dehydration can cause. If you wish, burn an incense or heat an oil like patchouli or eucalyptus, something earthy or with a sharp tang to it to bring you back to this reality.

Totems and the Inner Journey

Totems are excellent for inner pathworking, particularly when dealing with our own more mammalian and reptilian traits. Some humans have a tendency to try to distance themselves from their biological urges (just look at the mixed messages we get about sex!). The problem with this practice is that the more we deny our animal selves, the more strongly those traits will fight the repression. The key to being able to use different aspects of our psychology is to embrace them rather than fight them, so that those aspects are no longer our enemies, but our allies.

Primary and secondary totems are particularly adept at showing us our inner nature. Through working with my primary totem, Wolf, I have learned much about what Timothy Leary first described as the second circuit of consciousness, the anal-territorial emotional circuit (Prometheus Rising — 1983/Wilson/p. 39-60).

This circuit deals with the patterns of dominance and submission, aggression and passivity, in human behavior. These patterns are a way of life for many wild canines–the structure of a wolf pack, for example, is based the explicit interaction between dominant and submissive wolves and the acceptance and/or shifting of these roles. If that dynamic were to disappear, the pack would disintegrate into disorder.

Primates still carry that same pack dynamic, whether we

admit to being primates or not. It is often a much more subtle thing in human society, unspoken, yet almost clichéd in our acceptance of having superiors in the workplace, the scholastic arena, even in the home. As much as some may praise egalitarianism we're a long way from completely embracing it.

I had trouble for years acting in any sort of a directly dominant manner. I was classically passive-aggressive, the embodiment of what transformational psychology terms "hostile weakness." Though I was frustrated by being thrust into submissive roles in everyday life I had a tendency to simply complain and fret rather than actually do anything about it. Deep down inside I felt that I was a horrible person while everyone else must have had some reason to be better than I was.

A couple of years ago I started working with the Eight Circuit model via *Prometheus Rising*, which offers a number of exercises to demonstrate the concepts discussed. I was able to take the concepts of the second circuit from Robert Anton Wilson's writing and combine them with my understanding of wolf pack dynamics to better evaluate my own behavior. I saw how my resentment of being placed in an Omega role, when what I really wanted to be was an Alpha, was preventing me from actually acting upon it. I examined each interaction with other people, how the dominance played out in each, and thereby was able to figure out how I could shift my behavior to gain an advantage in each situation. Because I acted so much like a wolf because of my bond with that animal, I was able to reprogram myself according to that section of my nature and benefit from it.

A somewhat more detailed description of my aspecting work can be found in chapter 5. In addition, an even more complete essay "Totems and Transformation: Psychological Shapeshifting in the First and Second Circuits," will be appearing in the upcoming anthology, *Magic on the Edge*, from Immanion Press.

Totems and Practical Magic

Animal totems can be superb aides in mundane, everyday magic. Many of our needs correspond to the needs of animals–food, shelter, sex, survival and companionship. Thus their lessons are easily adaptable to our unique problems. Tertiary totems in particular seem suited for this sort of magic due to their transitory nature; primary and secondary totems are generally more focused on internal metamorphosis and personality-based issues.

As stated previously, you'll need to determine which totem to call on for your need. I've had success several times working with Beaver and Otter in tandem for job-related magic. The former helps me to find an occupation that's productive and rewarding, while the latter pushes for a job that has some entertainment for me and also reminds me to take time out to play. Smaller animals that hoard food, such as Squirrel or Ant, are excellent for financial issues and frugality. If you live in an unsafe neighborhood and can't move right away try calling on Dog or Wolf for protection.

Farewell, My Friend

Eventually you will find it's time to say farewell to your tertiary, secondary, and in certain cases, primary totems. This is normal. Once the totem has taught you all s/he has to teach, s/he will move on. In some cases the relationship may not be working out; perhaps you've been working with a tertiary that's not as appropriate for your need as you initially thought. Just perform a hail and farewell ritual. Make a final offering, let the totem know you've appreciated hir efforts and let hir know what you have learned from hir.

Sometimes the goodbye isn't forever; at times a totem may deem it necessary to back out of your life for a while, or you may ask hir to give you some space. Again, there is no problem here; it happens all the time. As with a final terminus, have a bit of a celebration in the totem's honor and reassure hir that hir time with you has been appreciated. Tell stories of the achievements and honors of your totem. Hold a feast for hir with some of hir favorite foods. Create a work of art depicting hir in a favorable manner. Let hir know that hir efforts have not gone unappreciated.

Chapter 2
Familiars

Most of the historical information on familiars comes from European and American witchcraft, in particular, from information gathered during the Inquisition and the Salem witch trials. The accused witches had demons in the form of animals with "unholy" names like Greedigut, Vinegar Tom and Pyewackett.

Michael Dalton, a 17th-century New England legal writer, had this to say on the discovery of familiars: "These witches have ordinarily a familiar or spirit...in the shape of a man, woman, boy, dog, cat, foal, hare, rat, toad, etc...Their said familiar hath some big or little teat upon their [the witch's] body, and in some secret place, where he sucketh [feeds] them"(Witches of the Atlantic World - 2000/*Dalton*/p. 366). Supposed gifts from Satan, these animals served the witches by aiding them in magical acts, transporting them to sabbats and loaning the human being their animal form for a time.

At the height of each localized witch craze, any household pet, or even a hapless animal found near the accused witch's home, would be "proof" of diabolical goings-on. Odd superstitions arose surrounding these creatures. For instance, a dog was suspected of being the familiar to several of the Salem witches. A rye cake made with the victims' urine was fed to the dog, the theory being that the canine would then speak the names of the guilty parties (Witches of the Atlantic World — 2000/*Breslaw*/p. 446). It's unknown as to whether or not Fido pleaded the Fifth.

Non-Eurocentric familiar animals were quite common, too, and their function was very much like that of the Eurocentric familiar. As noted in the totemism chapter, southeast Australian magical practitioners had a very familiar-like bond with a particular species, and examples of physical animals were shown to be indicative of hir abilities. Like European witches, those in many African tribes are said to ride upon various animals – owls, antelopes, snakes and leopards in particular. Also, the African witches reportedly take the forms of their familiars in their travels. And the animals often perform tasks for their human compatriots.

Putting it into Practice

I'll admit it–when I first started planning this book I had had no practical experience with familiars. Almost all of the animals that had shared my home since I began practicing magic as a teenager had been too flighty to really focus on such things. The ferrets were mostly interested in stealing things, the dogs were too distracted by interesting scents and ritual objects they oughtn't touch, and for various reasons I was never able to have a cat of my own. The animals I shared my home with once I started practicing magic were pets, and as pets they were fantastic; the only one who seemed capable of familiar status– a ball python–died before I could really work with her.

The existing information specific to physical animal familiars is rather scarce. Most of it involves anecdotes of pets that seem to be attracted to ritual activity (or at least to the humans participating), or bits and pieces of old witchcraft trials listing familiar species and names. Now, this book is for practicing magic-users, and it wouldn't make much sense to have a chapter solely on theory. In addition I'd wanted to try familiar magic for quite some time, and the opportunity finally arose. So I set out to find a familiar.

Many sources would have you believe that you always have to wait for a familiar to come to you. I didn't have that luxury, partially because of my timelines and partially because I needed an animal that fit my lifestyle, so I wanted to take a more active participation in the search than a general "help wanted" ritual.

I spent several weeks giving thought and energy to the idea, building the intent in my mind until I felt it was ready to release it into action. I didn't think about specific types of animals other than the practicality of something that would be happy in a relatively confined area, given my one-bedroom-apartment status. I didn't do too much formal work; rather, I used a form of trance I get into when I go for long walks and focused the energy from those walking meditations into my quest.

I also emphasized the need for a familiar that would be an active and equal participant in ritual. Most of the examples of familiar animals I found in modern practice involved someone's dog that would "guard the door during ritual" or cats "that always come running when I cast a circle." I definitely wanted a familiar willing to keep an eye on things while I was in altered states of consciousness, but I also wanted to be able to ask for active aid with magical work. I wanted a familiar that would be a partner as well as a guardian and general source of animal energy and inspiration.

I ended up with Tatzelwurm, a lovely ocellated skink, named after a mythical giant lizard reportedly living in the Alps (Unexplained — 1993/*Clark*/p. 360-361). She's quite practical–she lives in a sand substrate in a roomy tank, so she's easy to clean up after. She eats mealworms and she makes absolutely no noise. She's incredibly solitary–she's living up to her namesake's cryptozoological shyness. She was perfect for my need at the time.

A Non-lethal Hunt

There are some practical points to consider. How urgently do you need the help? How active do you want the familiar to be in your workings–do you just want one who will hang out and add to the natural ambience, or do you want a familiar who will contribute hir own effort to the task in exchange for a gift? Are you comfortable with evoking a familiar's energy, or do you view the practice as immoral? (Again, I remind you to make your own decisions in regards to ethics.) If you're a stickler for elemental magic, is the animal's natural element one that you're comfortable working with? Remember, some have more than one element; ducks, for instance, are mobile in the air, in water, and on land.

More mundanely, it is imperative that you analyze your physical life in detail. Remember–this is a physical, living, breathing animal you're taking into your home. Unlike totems and other noncorporeal beings, domestic animals must have your assistance to survive on this plane of existence. It is an act of responsibility, and if you are not completely sure you can provide the necessary care, I highly recommend passing on familiar magic until your situation has changed so that you can accommodate the familiar's needs.

Is your home large enough for a free-roaming animal? Can you afford food, veterinary bills and other daily care? If you're considering a dog or cat, can you pay for spaying or neutering? If there's a medical emergency can you cover the expenses? Do you live with anyone who is allergic to or frightened by certain species? What are the federal, state and local laws on keeping certain animal as pets? For instance, ferrets and many other exotics are illegal to own in California and New York City but not in other places. Wild animals are generally illegal to posses anywhere without a license.

Do you have enough time to dedicate to the animal's physical, psychological and emotional needs? This is very important. Mammals and birds, as well as certain reptiles like iguanas, are high maintenance in this respect. Boredom can cause ill health and destruction of your home, belongings or even the animal itself. Unhappy animals also tend to be less friendly to people—do you really want an antisocial creature in your home, causing tension and potentially endangering other occupants? Are you better off looking for smaller lizards, snakes or even hermit crabs while bypassing the ferrets, dogs and twenty-foot-long burmese pythons? Does the animal in question do better alone or in groups, and are you able to take care of multiple creatures if the latter is true? How will the animal react to other pets in your home?

Will the familiar require more mundane training, such as obedience classes? I have heard people claim that such things will break a familiar's will. I strongly disagree with this viewpoint. Familiars need to know as much as pets about things like not running out into the street and getting hit by a car, not eating the poisonous houseplants (which should be out of reach anyway) and even not getting on the furniture if that's your preference. They also need to be thoroughly socialized with humans and other animals to avoid future tension and to create a happier environment for everyone involved. Being a familiar is no excuse for an animal to be ill-behaved and thereby putting hirself and/or others in peril. They may be more magically adept and easier to train due to their intelligence, but they don't come with an inherent understanding of human rules, and expecting otherwise is a disaster waiting to happen!

When you set out on your search, whether you preface it with a ritual or simply step out the door with intent, keep in mind that you are seeking a familiar, not a pet. You may want to be able to do simple divination, whether intuitively or with a small tool like a pendulum or a coin.

Intuition, in fact, can be a key tool in determining your familiar. Some people find that when they meet their familiar for the first time that there is a moment of "Ah, yes, *there* you are!" Or it may be a bit more subtle, a continual draw back to that particular creature or a persistent feeling of "rightness." This initial impression is usually confirmed once the magician and the familiar begin working together.

Most cities have pet stores. I advise avoiding the big-box chains, as the health of their animals is dubious. Find a smaller, independent retailer—generally the owner will know more about the sources of the animals as well as care advice. Be sure, with birds and reptiles, to ask if an animal has been wild-caught or captive-bred—the latter will be healthier and better adjusted to captivity. In addition, illegal trade in endangered species for pets threatens the survival of these animals in the wild.

For dogs, cats, rabbits and ferrets, I highly recommend

visiting local animal shelters and breed rescues. Not only will you be saving the life of an animal that may otherwise have been euthanized, but it's easier to find adult animals which may be more effective and practical for your particular situation.

Wild animals, with rare exception, do NOT make good familiars, at least not as indoor animals. They are not accustomed to human company or confinement, and the stress of forced domestication will invariably negate any magical aid they may offer. Don't assume, for instance, that the baby bunnies you found in the grass on your search are your new little fuzzy familiars. Chances are that the mother left them there in hiding (or so she assumed) and will be back soon to care for them. Don't romanticize the situation and therefore ruin everybody's day. Do not encourage a wild animal that hangs around your home—that raccoon may be adorable sitting in the tree outside your window, but if s/he starts expecting food after the first handout s/he may become even more vehement about digging in your garbage for treats, and if s/he loses hir fear of humans may even be bold enough to bite! In addition, if you see a wild animal wandering near humans in a decidedly uncharacteristic manner there's a good chance s/he's got rabies, a disease certainly not conducive to anyone's plans, magical or mundane.

Some animals tend to do better in multiples—be sure to ask whoever's aiding you in your selection about this. Ferrets, for one, often get sold individually, but tend to live better in groups of two or more. Certain reptiles, amphibians and fish are also social creatures. Dogs are highly social animals, too, and many cats can adjust well to living in a colony. Not every animal you bring under your roof will be a familiar, but the one (or more) that is may very well thrive better with a companion of hir own species.

Make sure when you bring home your new companion that you always offer the following indoors or out–food, water, shelter and shade. These are required by law in most areas, and for good reason. Food and water are obvious. Shelter and shade are particularly important for outdoor or indoor/outdoor animals, like dogs and cats. It's no fun being stuck out in the rain or snow, and animals are as susceptible to becoming ill or dying from exposure as humans.

If you have animals already living in your home give them all some time to adjust to the newcomer, and vice versa. If there's just no safe compatibility–for instance, your pet cat isn't going to respect your familiar rat as anything but food–be certain that you can keep both/all animals safely away from each other.

I do have a few personal pet peeves (no pun intended) regarding animal care. Keep in mind that these are my personal viewpoints that I feel the need to voice. First off, dogs are much better off, if they have to be outdoors all day, in a fenced-in area rather than on a chain. Fences offer an easily definable boundary, whereas tugging against a chain becomes very frustrating because the dog can SEE the wide area ahead and can't figure out why s/he can't get there. Also, a dog in a fence feels more able to run away from threats whereas the chained dog has the binding holding hir in place—and s/he knows it. This very commonly breeds aggression in the dog. Keep in mind, I'm talking about dogs that live outdoors a great deal of the time; letting your indoor lapdog out on a chain for fifteen minutes is a lot different from tying a dog to a post day in and day out.

I also dislike seeing cats roaming outdoors. Sure, they're independent, and they usually come home regularly, but they are in much greater danger than an indoor cat, who doesn't have to worry nearly as much about strange dogs, cars or sadistic humans. Additionally, they can become a real nuisance to neighbors—I remember one of my dogs was regularly tormented by neighborhood cats that would sit just outside the fence and actively taunt him.

If you must let your cat outside, I highly suggest allowing hir to keep hir claws. Declawing not only leaves the cat without hir first defense, but it also involves removing the entire first joint of the front toes, which can cause balance issues and pain long after the outer wounds have healed. Imagine going through life without your fingertips. And while we're on the subject of unnecessary body part removals, let me just say that as a former veterinary technician, watching the process of day-old puppies having their tails chopped off without anesthesia was one of the most traumatizing sights in that career. I can only be glad I didn't have to witness ear cropping. Enough said.

Finally, let me say that I very, very strongly advocate spaying or neutering all dogs and cats, be they familiars or not. Thousands of unwanted animals are put to death every year because their forebears' owners didn't follow this common medical practice. Fixing an animal won't cause it to miss its reproductive capabilities. They're hormonally caused, and if the hormones aren't there, there's no urge to mate. It also lessens the chances of certain types of cancer and other ailments. The surgery is done with anesthesia and is routine to the point of it being an outpatient procedure in most clinics.

Familiars and Magical Acts

As with any other magical partner, the relationship with a familiar is an individual one. Much of what is presented here is what I learned in my interaction with Tatzel. With this, like all magic, you have the freedom to explore to find what works best for you.

Give the familiar a few months to adjust to hir new setting. Get into a routine to make hir comfortable, and get to know each other on a perfectly mundane basis. Don't get discouraged if s/he's not leaping into your arms every time you walk into the room. Some animals just aren't as expressive as others. I'm happy if I get to see Tatzel once a day–most of the time she's happily burrowing underneath the surface of her sand substrate. This also teaches you to notice when s/he may not be feeling well, which may simply mean s/he's not up for magic, or that s/he may need medical attention. Knowing your familiar on a companion basis is as rewarding as having hir as a magical partner.

Once s/he's settled in, it's time to make sure s/he is your familiar, and that s/he's ready for the role. In a ritual format, communicate with hir intuitively or with a divination tool as to whether s/he is willing to be your familiar; then double-check with divination to be sure that s/he truly is ready. If s/he is, you need to work out between the two of you what tasks s/he will be helping with, what sort of gifts you'll give hir for hir help, and so on.

When I did my dedication ritual to Tatzel, we talked quite a bit about our relationship. She even gave me enough of a lizard-boost that I did a minor shapeshifting dance afterwards. I'm sure I looked positively ridiculous lying on my stomach and dragging myself around with my arms, but I did get a taste of her means of locomotion despite my inadequate body. I then passed to her a bit of the sensation of what it is to have a human body ("You have no scales! How do you protect yourself?" she exclaimed).

I found it necessary to create a protective bond between Tatzel and me; I wanted to help keep her safe while she did her side of the magical work. Her preference is to receive her directions in ritual, then work on it all evening once the ritual is done. She's very much a long-time and long-patience familiar. I didn't want her to be vulnerable during the process so I used a candle to carry my blessing on her. I chose a red votive candle for Fire, as that is a representative element of this desert lizard, carved her name, a small lizard, and the rune *elhaz* on the top of it, and added a bit of my hair and her sand substrate (You can also use bits of the familiar's fur, feathers or shed skin.). If your familiar wears a collar, you might attach a small charm for protection or magical enhancement to the collar—make sure it's something that won't snag, like the animal's rabies or ID tags.

Some people like to give their familiars an alternate name in addition to their everyday one, the same as many human magicians have "working" names for themselves. While it isn't necessary, it won't hurt. The rosters of witchcraft trials may be used, or mythological beings, or whatever you choose. The familiar may very well have a name for hirself—try asking. Just don't use the magical name in everyday parlance, especially in any obedience training, so as to avoid confusion on the part of both the familiar and other people in regular contact with you both. Opinions vary as to whether the magical name should be used regularly in private. Some say that doing so erodes the subconscious magical association of the name; others find that it actually strengthens the familiar relationship for the human to refer to the familiar with the magical name.

Discuss this with your familiar, to see what s/he thinks.

There are several advantages to sharing one's ritual space with an animal familiar. The general energy particular to the species adds a certain flavor to the work. Tatzel, being a desert lizard, adds to any Earth or Fire based magic. She's also good at long-shot magic, given that animals in the desert must learn to conserve resources in order to survive. In metamorphic magic she's an excellent teacher of hind-brain instincts and focusing on basic needs. Simple observation reveals that some days it really does come down to food, water, shelter and shade, and I've learned better appreciation of these things from her.

I also regularly ask her for protection along with the rest of my routine evocations whenever I begin a ritual. Her tank sits right by the door to the ritual room and she always seems quite happy to keep an eye open. I'll rarely see her except at feeding-time, but I know she's there.

Familiars can be used for divination purposes. If the animal has a regular feeding schedule, offer one portion of food per possible answer to your question; whatever portion the animal approaches first is the most likely outcome. You can also play "Groundhog Day" with more reserved familiars; ask a question of the familiar, then state that if s/he shows hirself within a certain period of time it will mean such-and-such answer.

Certain familiars may charge magical items. A small mojo pouch can be tied to the collar of a dog or cat. A candle or other object may be placed in the tank of a smaller creature. These apply only if the items are nontoxic–never assume the animal won't chew on them. Critters will go after the strangest things, and unfortunately they don't discern between poisonous/harmful and safe.

A familiar may be evoked in otherworldly journeying for protective and/or guidance purposes, similar to the traditional animal spirit guide. S/he may also be given independent magical tasks to perform with a reward of a treat of some sort if they are completed to the best of hir ability (remember, everyone has misses as well as successes!)

Evocation, when used with a physical being, allows communication that cannot happen on a physical level. You can sit and verbally instruct your piebald rat in magic all day, but I doubt much will come of it. Evocation allows the practitioner to communicate with the animal on a more spiritual level–it connects with the species-specific essence (in other words, the energy) of that individual animal. Think of it as somewhat along the lines of the concept of the Higher Self. It's a bit different from conventional evocation. It's not so much a matter of calling a spirit into your ritual area as it is inviting your physical familiar to take active part in the magic. I tend to not to try to separate any aspect of a physical being's spirit from hir body without permission–after all, you wouldn't want to suddenly find your consciousness skewed, would you? If the familiar is willing, you can invoke hir energy into you, as I did with my initiation ritual with Tatzel when I became a lizard for a while, as well as give the animal a piece of yourself if s/he so desires.

This also allows the familiar to clearly accept or reject a request, just like any other entity one may work with, corporeal or not. I don't see asking a familiar for help as any more coercive than making the same query of a totem or a deity. Whether or not all this translates into physical behavior depends on the individual familiar. The keynote of success, as with all magic, is whether the desired result is achieved in the end.

Some people claim that all familiars communicate through telepathy. This, of course, assumes that the human in question is telepathic. I myself am about as responsive as a stone when it comes to mental instant messaging. My familiar, Tatzel, tends to be pretty quiet about things; while she does have a tendency to show herself quite a bit during my more Nature-based rituals I've yet to have her indicate anything otherwise beyond annoyance if I try to handle her too much. I certainly haven't received any telepathic messages from her, not that I've noticed anyway. This doesn't mean it's not possible; it just means that it's not a requirement for effective familiar magic. My track record with her, which is overwhelmingly good, attests to this.

If you're really worried about miscommunication, use a simple divination tool like a pendulum and some yes/no questions to check your work. You can both ask the familiar questions directly, using the tool for translation, and periodically refocus yourself by asking the tool if you're still communicating with the familiar or just with your own wishful thinking. If you start getting garbled messages it's a good sign you need to take a break.

Living With the Magic

Apart from the magic, it's just more pleasant having another living being in my home, one who doesn't come with all the baggage and bullshit of a human being. The glimpses I get of her when she ventures out at night or when I clean her tank delight me uncontrollably, bringing back memories of my childhood nature rambles. The red glow of her heat lamp has become a comforting night-light and reminds me that even at the worst of times I'm not alone.

The mealworms I feed her, too, have not gone without teaching me as well. They've been a reminder that even the smallest creatures deserve my humane treatment. Although they come into my life to feed Tatzel, in the meantime they are offered sustenance and shelter. When the time comes to feed the lizard I am also reminded of the continual cycles of life, death and rebirth, not only in their most literal form but also in the more symbolic and abstract patterns that permeate everyday life.

Even if an animal you bring into your life turns out to be a spectacularly awful familiar, the simple joy of the company of a nonhuman animal can be rewarding in and of itself, and the ability to live in the moment is a lesson we can all benefit from, magician or no.

Spiritual Familiars

Obviously, for some people having a physical animal in the home isn't a viable option. Whether space, time, allergies, or finances complicate the issue, these magicians can still enjoy the relationship with a familiar animal on a nonphysical level.

I have a number of animal spirits that roam my home. Many of them are a result of the various animal parts that I use in ritual; others simply seem to be attracted to the ambient energy of my living space. I leave my place welcome to all if they will do no harm to me and mine. Most of the time they're content to remain in the background; I don't call any of them by any names, nor do I ask much more of them beyond simply being at peace while living with me. They aren't required to stay, but can come and go as they please.

It's gotten to the point where I sort of have my own spiritual ecosystem in my personal space. I've built up a certain ambient energy over the years which these spirits seem to enjoy, and in turn their presence build on and enhances that ambience. I have both an environment and the denizens therein. In fact, every time I move I carry this combined energy in a special clay vessel I made years ago. I invite all of them to come with me or stay behind as they prefer, and for those that stay I remind them that they always have a home with me.

I do call upon them in ritual. In my routine evocations I call upon them as my friends, family and guardians, and as those who have aided me in various ways in the past. Again, I don't normally ask them to complete specific tasks for me, but simply to add to the wild energy of the ritual space and time.

A lot of the methods I use in building relationships with totems also work quite nicely for inviting individual animal spirits into my life. In fact, these are excellent exercises regardless of what area of animal magic you're working with.

Over the years I have attuned my own energy to the characteristics that make me an animal. After all, *Homo sapiens* is a mammal, and we share varying amounts of genetic material with all animals. Awareness of those parts of us that are biologically programmed allows us to use them more wisely and to not let them control us. It also is an advantage in animal magic, particularly in making yourself a more comfortable presence to various animal entities.

I have also made my home quite attractive to animal spirits. Each picture, statue, book and work of my own art is a miniature offering to Nature as a whole and adds its own energy to that which pervades my home. Each reinforces my own connection to the world of fauna and serves as a message to all visitors that this place is sacred to animals. In short, the spirits just seem to like my home décor, and it is enhanced by their

83

presence.

You don't have to turn your living space into a shrine to animals to work with spiritual familiars, nor do you need to fully embrace your wild nature. It is a good idea, though, to enhance the natural energy around you. First, make sure your home is relatively clean; most healthy animals will not willingly live in their own filth. Keep yourself clean and healthy as well; many animals will avoid others that are ill or injured.

To enhance your own animal energy, try to become more like an animal. Internalizing the influence of a totem animal helps a great deal. Even if you don't have a primary or secondary totem you can ask a tertiary totem for help with this. You can choose an animal with whom you feel some kinship, or try working with an animal traditionally associated with shapeshifting such as Wolf, Jaguar, Hare or Raven.

Work with the totem every day. Meditate on hir qualities and work with hir, and perhaps even try some shapeshifting rituals. Begin to see yourself as that animal. As you walk around, imagine what it would be like to be moving as that species. Try to see the world through the eyes of the totem animal you're working with. Be focused—you should only work with one totem to maximize the impact of your work, unless whoever you're working with indicates otherwise.

The more work you do with the totem, the more integrated that animal energy will become in your being. This aids in your understanding of the animal mindset, which makes communication with animal spirits that much easier.

Decorating your home with animal images again not only shows your respect for the animals themselves, but also reminds you of what you're focusing on magically. In addition, some animal spirits like to take up a sort of residence in images and icons of their own species. As discussed in Chapter 6, most animal parts already have a spirit attached to them. I've also had spirits decide to adopt statues, paintings and other depictions of animals; a few are even attracted to my books!

I prefer to allow such visitors to arrive organically; I don't call for them. If you'd like to send out a spiritual signal that you'd like some company, however, there are definitely some options. Try purifying any images of animals you might have and do a ritual dedicating them as a spirit-home. Make offerings of food available; if you seek a specific type of animal, be sure to tailor your offerings to their preferences. You may want to keep the offering open-ended, though, and definitely don't leave them where real animals might get a hold of them–most animals, from household pets to suburban wildlife, are opportunistic feeders! You can also build up the natural energy of your home with houseplants and pets–properly cared for, of course. You don't have to indulge in all of these methods, especially if all you want is one or two familiars. The benefits of ambient animal energy are often worth the effort in and of themselves.

If you want to be more direct, perform a ritual evoking

a familiar spirit into your life. Don't be specific; rather, state your desires and allow the magic to do the rest. As with physical familiars it's a good idea to leave things relatively open-ended so that you get the familiar you need, not necessarily the one you think you need. There are more possibilities, of course. One's spiritual familiar need not be a domestic housepet. Wildlife and even fantastic creatures have aided magicians as long as magicians have been around. With spiritual familiars it's possible to receive aid from a tiger, a lemur, or even a basilisk!

You'll know when your familiar arrives. You may catch glimpses in your peripheral vision, or hear odd, out-of-place noises. If you're at all sensitive to energy you'll notice a decided addition. Familiars may also try to communicate through dreams, though again, as with totems, be careful in your judgment of subconscious messages.

Again, as with physical familiars, give yourself some time to get acquainted with the spirit. Ask hir name, or name hir if s/he prefers. Ask hir why s/he decided to answer your call and what s/he'd like out of the relationship. See if s/he'd like an icon for a home, and what sort of offerings s/he'd like in exchange for magical help. Find out if s/he's ever worked magic before, and if so, what type. Also, study hir species as you would a totem to determine what sort of magic would be good for experimentation.

The rest of the material that applies to physical familiars, with the exception of daily care considerations, should also be taken into account. In addition, as spiritual familiars do not have a physical form that the magician needs to take care of, the concept of a lifespan within the working relationship is quite different in this situation. Don't allow yourself to think that a spiritual familiar is any less respect worthy because of this, though. While such entities tend to be more autonomous than their fleshly counterparts they're not toys to be placed in a box when you're through with them. Let them know they are appreciated and you'll get much better results overall.

If all else fails, you can even create a spiritual familiar—Chapter 4 details this process.

Lupa

Chapter 3
Animal-based Evocation and Invocation

Evocation and invocation do not always occur on a totemic level. The energies and personae of both anthropomorphized and natural animals have been a subject of magical theory and practical experimentation for centuries.

Some spring directly from earlier totemic systems, animal symbols of directions being a good example. Others, such as fantastic animals like the basilisk and dragon, were derived in part from exaggerations and tall tales surrounding perfectly mundane animals as well as alleged encounters on various planes of existence. Regardless of origin, these more-than-ordinary animals are excellent allies in magical work, and often have quite a bit of information to impart if they are dealt with properly.

Invocation, in addition, is an excellent way to better understand the self. The study of any full pantheon soon reveals a complete spectrum of the human psyche. When you invoke a member of that pantheon, not only are you working with the external deity, but also the corresponding part of yourself. This can be especially useful when performing metamorphic magics, such as strengthening weaker aspects of your personality. Totemism is a form of animal magic perfectly suited for such work.

89

Evoking Elements and Quarters in Animal Form

One of the earliest portions of my practice involved discovering which animals represented each of the four cardinal directions for me. Between a mix of intuition and a smattering of assorted indigenous lore (some of which, in retrospect, was probably rather dubious in source) I found the critters that worked best for me. There's been some shifting in the ranks since then, but I've come up with a system that, all flaws in derivation aside, works very well for me.

Black Wolf has always been North to me. She brings with her lush green forests and cool, damp earth beneath my paws. White Hawk ever dances in the East in the yellow sunlight and gives me wings to wear during ritual.

In the yellow West I have two bears; after I read *Giving Voice to Bear* by David Rockwell, in which people of cultures worldwide were described as referring to Bear through euphemisms, I was inspired ask their names. The female grizzly is Grandmother Silverclaw, while the male black bear is Grandfather Silvertip, or so they told me. The former brings in healing energies and the latter takes away that which harms.

South, the direction of Fire and therefore Change, naturally has seen the most shifting in symbolism. South has always been represented by the color red, but the space has been filled over the years by Buffalo, Elk, Horse, Cat and Fox. South usually represents whatever changes I'm currently going

90

through, and the animal is that which best aids me with that stage.

When seeking animals to evoke for each quarter, keep in mind what each one represents to you. The animal should embody those traits. Don't choose an animal just because it's deemed proper by someone else.

You may try meditating at each quarter with a separate ritual for each. The guided meditation in Appendix A may be modified in intent for this purpose. In fact, most, if not all, of the material in the totemism chapter may be adapted for use with directional animals.

There was a brief period where I attempted to change all four directional animals at once with no real reason, which didn't go over well at all. I tried using the traditional Wiccan view of the directions and elements and chose animals that seemed like they should fit into those spaces. After working with the new setup for a few rituals I found that it just didn't feel right to me, as clichéd as that may sound. So I went back to the animals that spoke to me before. I've been happy with them ever since. This taught me that the best avenue in determining directional animal correspondences is best done through experience and trial-and-error, not necessarily what someone else says is best.

Animal-based Deity-forms and Other Mythological Personae

The majority of polytheistic deities have some form of animal associated with them. Whether the deity is humanoid or not, the animal is still a symbol of that particular entity. Often hir culture's mythos will explain the link between the divine and the primal.

Many people are familiar with the gods of the Egyptian pantheon, most of whom possess the heads of animals native to the area. While more abstract than totems, many of these deities still carry some of their animal avatar's traits. As stated in *The Egyptian Book of Living and Dying* by Joann Fletcher, "The animals linked with a particular deity featured prominently in his or her worship but were not themselves the object of veneration–they were revered as manifestations of the deity, or as embodiments of divine characteristics" (The Egyptian Book of Living and Dying — 2002/*Fletcher*/ p. 74).

Anyone who has spent any time around cats and found it to be a rewarding experience will have no trouble understanding why Bast, goddess of love, pleasure and protection of crops, is a feline deity. Cats are inherently graceful and even a bit hedonistic, but in a charming manner. And the original domestic felines of the area proved themselves to be invaluable in protecting grain and other food from rats, mice and other vermin. Bast is a supreme example of personification of animal traits.

Anubis, a deity very intimately associated with death and the mummification process, has the head of a jackal. Like many canines, jackals became symbols and avatars of death due to their tendency to scavenge battlefields and graveyards for the meat the dead provided.

The Norse deities also have strong ties to their animal symbols. Odin is famous for his two wolves and his pair of ravens, as well as Sleipnir the eight-legged horse. The one-eyed god also takes on the form of an eagle at times. Bast is echoed in Freya's attraction to cats. Thor, on the other hand, travels frequently in a cart drawn by a pair of goats. Freyr's boar has long been a symbol of good fortune, especially in times of conflict and war.

The Greeks, too, assigned animals to their pantheon, and often combined them with a minor creation tale. Artemis has an entire entourage—most wild animals are hers, though the bear and the deer are particularly emblematic of the huntress. Athena has as her standard the owl, and is responsible for the existence of the spider through the transformation of the weaver Arachne. Poseidon, in turn, provided humanity with the great aid of the horse, an animal said to still run within the white caps of the waves. Like Odin, Zeus is associated with the eagle, though he also took the form of a swan and a bull in his questionable liaisons with mortal women. His wife, Hera, is particularly fond of the vain peacock; the many eyes were placed there after their original owner, Argus, was killed while guarding one of Zeus' flings, Io (incidentally herself transformed into a heifer).

A number of non-deific personalities that may be drawn from in Greek mythology as individual entities or as archetypes also have rich animal histories. Aside from the previously-mentioned Arachne and Io one may also find Callisto, the nymph Artemis changed into the Great Bear (aka the Big Dipper) and Actaeon, transformed into a stag and torn apart by his own hounds. There are also animal-human hybrids such as centaurs, satyrs and the Gorgons, not to mention animal hybrids like Pegasus and the Chimera.

Many Native American story cycles involve personalities that have animal names, but often take human form. Not purely totemic or deific, they nonetheless are strong personifications of animal energies and are incredibly primal and close to their sources. Entire social structures are sometimes created around them, for they marry one another and interact on a daily basis for good or for ill. Their tales demonstrate favorable and unfavorable behavior for the cultures that tell them.

Coyote stories are among some of the most colorful, and while often simple in their structure, they hide quite a bit of knowledge for those willing to study them in depth. Coyote is the epitome of the trickster archetype and has absolutely no shame. He is undiluted Chaos, raw energy and naiveté mixed with wisdom. He often falls into his own traps, but like the infamous Wile E. Coyote of Warner Brothers fame he's always popping back up in the next frame. One can learn much about resilience and adaptability just from the tales told of this character. Barry Holstun Lopez's *Giving Birth to Thunder, Sleeping With His Daughter* is a superior collection of Coyote tales.

Anthropomorphized animals are also found within the well-known Aesop's fables. Like many indigenous stories, these short parables allow animal energies to personify personality traits and the interactions thereof. While some of the stereotypes aren't quite based on actual animal behavior so much as human assumptions thereof, nonetheless they are a valuable resource when seeking animal-based entities to work with.

Some entities don't necessarily have an animal form, nor do they necessarily have the power of deities, but are still helpful when dealing with animal magic. Saint Francis of Assisi is a prime example. Whether or not you believe that this particular saint existed in this reality, the mythos that has arisen around him is still a good resource. The most famous tale tells of his taming a ravenous wolf that was plaguing the city of Gubbio, though he is well-known for his kindness and respect for all animals. This archetypal descendant of pagan deities also wrote the beautiful "Canticle of the Sun". Those who automatically shy away from Christian language would do well to read this highly pantheistic piece of writing lightly wrapped in God-speak. Substitute the deity-name of your choice for the word "Lord" and you have a beautiful bit of verse that may be integrated into any number of magical workings, particularly those dealing with nature.

The association of deities and others with animals is not always a purely positive one. Tyr, for instance, probably should not be evoked at the same time as Fenris due to his betrayal of the great wolf. Fenris himself is a powerful–though not entirely benign–entity in and of himself; the same goes for Jormungandr, the Midgard Serpent. They can be useful when properly focused, but care should be taken nonetheless; in other words, know what you're working with before you start the work. Be aware of any edgy or potentially conflicting traits when evoking or invoking any entity alone of in tandem with others. Bringing Apollo and Python into the same circle, for instance, may lead to less-than desirable results.

Be aware, too, that the associations of animals often become twisted from their natural origins, particularly in later sources. Medieval bestiaries, while providing a wealth of interesting writing about animals, both real and fantastic, are more often than not inaccurate. They also many times ascribe Christian-based morals to the beasts that may or may not have anything to do with an animal's behavior. This also carries over into fairy tales and later folklore, and any corresponding information from such sources should be used with caution–not that it isn't necessarily true to some aspect of the species, but if you intend to evoke Wolf, you may prefer a more natural archetype to the demonized version found terrorizing little girls in red capes and porcine siblings.

Fantastic Animals

Opinions vary as to whether or not fantastic animals should be considered totems or not. For the most part they can serve many of the same functions as totem animals. However, one of the characteristics of a totem animal is that it can teach us how to interact with our surroundings through being native to this world. In addition, one of the primary sources of totemic teachings is through observing physical animal behavior. Fantastic animals cannot do these things for us as they exist, depending on your source, either in ethereal planes or within the imagination alone.

This, of course, does not prevent utilizing their aid in magical work. Few people have witnessed deities, demons and devas in a physical form, yet many work with them on a regular basis.

The origin of these species varies according to individual mythology and culture, as well as how much literature is available for each. The unicorn is supposed to be an exaggeration of several different mundane horned animals, including the ibex and the rhinoceros. There is a wealth of information on origin theories for this popular beast, as well as associated lore. The chimera, on the other hand, has only one myth to her name, the one in which she is destroyed; little is known other than her origin, her general nature and her destruction. Factors contributing to these and other disparate histories probably range from country of origin to whether or not there was a physical animal resembling the fantastic one in question. Those whose supposed earthly forms could be observed collected quite a bit of exaggerated lore, while those that were primarily imaginative didn't have quite so much fodder to start with.

A few creatures gained much lore from fossilized or found remains. The best example of this is the dragon. Ancient cultures, upon discovering the gigantic bones of dinosaurs, embellished their findings with speculations of huge lizards roaming the earth. Spectacular talents such as the ability to breathe fire and flight were attributed to these half-true, half-mythical animals. On the other hand the long spiral tooth of the narwhal–a small whale little known to most non-seafarers until recently–was often sold at exorbitant prices as an alicorn, the single horn of the unicorn.

The individual practitioner must decide whether or not to disregard the totemic traits of the mundane animals that are the probable basis of many fantastic beasts. On the one hand these traits may help give a better understanding, especially for creatures lacking in lore. On the other hand, there is something to be said for allowing the mythos to stand alone.

Since there's precious little observation to be done in

person, the first place to start researching fantastic animals is by reading the mythology and literature surrounding them. The wonderful thing about magic is that you can work with creatures that have these seemingly absurd and impossible traits and create successful magic with them. So don't be turned away from the fire-resistant salamander just because the amphibian of the same name is flammable.

While there are excellent dictionaries and encyclopedias of mythological beasts, I recommend definitely consulting primary sources. Classical and world mythology is rife with creatures capable of everything from restoring youth to turning enemies to stone. Bestiaries, dating back to the works of Pliny and extending into medieval and even Renaissance times, elaborate on many of the more famous imaginative animals and generate some of the more outlandish traits.

Again, as with totems, you may want to directly ask the entity in question what s/he is capable of. Keep in mind that mythology is from a human perspective; even if these animals sprang directly from the human imagination, many of them have gained enough power over the years to become autonomous and may very well have developed beyond the initial descriptions. On the other hand, if they truly are autonomous beings native to other planes of existence it's almost certain that human observation has provided us with either incomplete and/or skewed results. In short, it helps to get up close and personal.

Extinct Animals

While extinct species no longer roam the same plane as we do, they still have the ability to work with us and to teach us what remains of their totemic and related lore. The more recently deceased are also a sad reminder of what is lost to us because of our irresponsibility–not only are the physical animals gone forever from our world, but they've taken many of their lessons with them. On the other hand, the discovery of a species once thought to be gone forever is a cause to celebrate, as it reopens access to an entire wealth of energy and knowledge previously spotty or even unattainable.

Longer-dead animals such as dinosaurs are also workable. While scientists have intuited a small portion of behavior of these and other long-dead creatures from fossil evidence, most likely the information on the animal will have to be supplemented with conversation with the animal spirit itself.

It's recommended that when working with extinct species that detailed notes are taken. There's a definite dearth of correspondences for these animals, and any consistent traits discovered through long-term work with them may be incredibly valuable for other practitioners down the line.

Cryptozoological Animals

Then there are the animals and animal-human hybrids of the field of cryptozoology, the creatures that may or may not exist in this physical world. As with fantastic and extinct animals, these enigmatic entities can't really teach much through direct observation of behavior. In fact, it's debatable as to whether or not any of them truly have ever existed in our world. Certainly some of the more outlandish ones such as the Jersey Devil and Mothman most likely belong to the realms of imagination and are, perhaps, exaggerations of glimpses of mundane creatures. Stranger things have happened, though–up until the late 1930's scientists were skeptical as to whether the giant panda bear even existed; it took the capture of a live specimen to shatter all myths. While the chances of bringing a genuine chupacabra in the flesh to light aren't that great, there is much speculation as to whether anomalous big cats seen in England and the supposedly extinct yet frequently sighted thylacine aren't just incredibly rare mundane animals.

Cryptids and fantastic beasts really only differ in the time period in which they have been sighted and in the methods used to try to prove or disprove their existence. Until the past two centuries much of the methodology used in mainstream science was based on superstition and erroneous observations. The field of cryptozoology, while far from being universally accepted by the scientific community and the public at large as a legitimate study, utilizes much more skepticism than the medieval observers of unicorns and dragons.

Regardless of whether a given cryptid exists, the mythology that builds up around it may be utilized in magic. After all, all mythology has at least some basis in the human imagination, and just because a being is newly birthed does not mean it is powerless. In fact it may be even more effective in that it has not stagnated and therefore is still capable of relatively rapid evolution in response to need.

As with fantastic animals, study up on cryptid lore (and be aware that some sources are incredibly sensationalized!) Many cryptids are characterized as being hostile towards humans, so be aware of potentially negative traits when choosing a cryptid to work with. Also, if a cryptid is an anomalous species sighted outside of its usual range or variation on a known species, it may be beneficial to study the mundane totemic qualities thereof.

On another note, if you happen to be a cryptozoologist yourself, you might want to try an evocation to affect a sighting of a cryptid. Magic is another field of study that is often scoffed at by scientists, but any serious practitioner willing to experiment knows that more often than not we are only limited by our focus and imagination.

Fictional Animals

Honestly, I'd never thought of working with supposedly fictional animal entities until I read Taylor Ellwood's *Pop Culture Magick*. After doing so, though, I came to the realization that pop culture–everything from film to anime to comic books and beyond–is simply today's mythology. These media offer a whole new realm of animal archetypes and characters to work with. After all, the deities and entities we have worked with for centuries, if not millennia, originally stemmed from human stories. The vehicle of communication may be more technologically sophisticated, but who is to say that it is any less valid?

My absolute, all-time favorite movie is Hayao Miyazaki's *Mononoke Hime* (*The Princess Mononoke.*) Within 134 minutes of stunningly executed animation and vivid storytelling is contained an entire new mythology powered by the attention and belief of millions who have seen it, many thousands of whom are devoted fans. Archetypes are not static; they constantly rebirth themselves in every culture that humans manage to create. As Ellwood states, "[P]op culture can appropriate the energy and concepts beyond these older god forms, or even systems of magic, and make something new out of them. We have modern archetypes that embody the energy of previous archetypes...some people will approach and understand magical practice better through pop culture as opposed to tradition" (Pop Culture Magic — 2004/*Ellwood*/p. 16).

Mononoke Hime is by far one of the most pagan-friendly modern stories. The setting involves a primordial deep forest populated by huge animal gods reminiscent of Campbell's Animal Masters, all deriving their ultimate source from the Great Forest Spirit, an entity resembling the famed cave-painted Shaman of Lascaux. In this modern-yet-timeless fable the energies of Nature work against the encroachment of human civilization in a number of manners. The Boars are bombastic warriors, blindly charging into a final battle in the hopes of destroying the enemy kamikaze-style. The Apes are pacifists, persistently replanting trees where humans have clearcut them and fleeing when they find they can no longer defend themselves. The Wolves use strategy and cunning with their smaller numbers, true to Wolf's totemic qualities in cultures at war. They are even resourceful to a high degree. Mirroring the wolf's eventual alliance with humans by evolving into the dog, Moro the Wolf Goddess adopts San when she was an abandoned baby and raises her to the point where the young girl becomes a bridge between the animal and human world. Yakul, the tame goat, represents domesticated totems in his partnership with Ashitaka, an exiled tribesman wandering the forest.

Pop Culture Magick details many ways in which entities in this movie and many other stories may be accessed similarly to more ancient paradigms. To overlook the value of our modern mythologies because they "aren't old enough" denies an incredible array of entities that have the power of modern-day belief behind them. Since there are always new stories being told in books, movies and on television, there isn't much chance of running out of new mythology anytime soon.

Taking a page out of Ellwood's work, I did a ritual working with entities from *Mononoke Hime*. First, I decided that the target of my attack would be Kills-the-Wolves, the force that causes humanity's unnatural hatred of that species and makes humans slaughter them unnecessarily (anyone who's read Barry Holstun Lopez' *Of Wolves and Men* knows what I'm talking about). It's the urge that makes people shoot them from airplanes, poison them, burn them alive and refuse to compromise–the thing that causes people to demonize the wolf in stories and legends. This isn't about our survival, but passes well beyond that into species hatred.

Obviously, I couldn't completely destroy this entity, but I could cause damage to it, so I created a sigil to represent the entity and placed the sigil on the top of a bucket filled with crumpled up newspaper. Next, I prepared my ritual area with routine evocations. I then put on my Mononoke costume that I made for anime conventions a few years ago, and then invoked myself into her (instead of invoking her into me), an idea taken directly from *Pop Culture Magick*. It was a very smooth invocation, a lot more fluid and thorough than some others I've done; part of this was probably due to my connection with the archetype, but some was also because of the method of invocation.

Then I evoked Moro, the Wolf Goddess, and her young. As a pack we circled the sigilized enemy, trapped in a circle of red. I stabbed the sigil with a spear several times, then proceeded to tear it to pieces with my teeth and claws, my pack aiding in the kill. I collected the pieces, burned some of them, and placed the rest in a bag to be burned over the next few days until nothing remained. I bid farewell to all who'd participated, and ended the ritual.

Overall, I'm very happy with how the ritual went. It was the first ritual magic I'd done involving pop culture entities, and just from this experience my suspicions were proven true–that a Wolf Goddess doesn't have to be millennia old to be powerful.

These are just a few examples of animal-based entities that may be called upon in magic and metamorphosis. Obviously, you're limited only by the imagination and observation of animals within all realms of existence.

Lupa

Chapter 4
Creating Animals in Magical Practice

Humans never seem to be quite satisfied with the natural fauna native to this plane of existence. Whether by enhancing the lore surrounding natural animals or by creating entirely new species out of thin air, we've managed to create a plethora of beasts we'll likely never see in the flesh.

I've already covered preexisting fantastic beasts in Chapter 3. This section will instead involve the creation of new composite animals and entirely new species, as well as fitting other entities with animal characteristics.

Composite Animals

Composite animals–those that are combinations of bits and parts of two or more species–pop up in mythology and folklore on a regular basis. Human-animal hybrids are popular, as are mixes of several types of animal, often very different in nature. Magically speaking, as a friend of mine put it, "Chimerical creatures are a way to have your cake and eat it too–lion or eagle? Have a gryphon."

The Greeks and other cultures came up with a number of composite animals. Centaurs are human above the waist, equine below. Pegasus is a large white horse with proportionate bird wings. The chimera is a strange mix of lion, goat and snake attributes–some descriptions give her three heads, while others simply divide her into thirds and assign a different animal to each section. The gryphon and sphinx both start with a lion base and add assorted other characteristics.

Medieval lore had a number of animals that supposedly had marine equivalents. The mermaid is the most famous aquatic hybrid. The narwhal is the basis for the watery version of the terrestrial unicorn. Hippocampi–horse/fish mixes–are often depicted drawing chariots of Poseidon and other ocean-based deities. And who can forget Capricorn, the sea-goat?

Even stranger animal hybrids exist than that. In one American Indian legend (tribe unspecified), the terrifying Flying Head was simply an enormous head with "Two huge bird wings [that] grew from either side of its cheeks, and with them it could soar into the sky or dive down, floating, like a buzzard" (Favorite Folktales from Around the World — 1986/Yolen/p. 234). Newer lore, stemming from remote American forestlands, offers some strange creatures. The fur-bearing trout supposedly developed hir pelt because of cold northern river temperatures–and tricky taxidermists sometimes turn an extra buck or two by providing "proof" of this critter's existence. Those same taxidermists are often sources of stuffed "jackalopes," rabbits with small deer antlers sprouting miraculously out of their heads.

European heraldry birthed some odd animals as well. The dragonnee is a mix of a dragon and a lion. The cockatrice is a wyvern (two-legged dragon) with a rooster's head. The harpy, originally from Greek mythology, appears in certain heraldic standards. The enfield combines features of the fox and wolf with the forelegs resembling the hind limbs of an eagle, and the yale (the animal, not the graduate–usually) is an odd mix of several hoofed animals and reportedly is able to pivot each individual horn as necessary. More familiar creatures like the dragon, the unicorn and the gryphon are seen again. The chimera is also present, though now with a human face added. In short, most of the mythical beasts found in heraldry are composite.

Now, obviously some of these creatures venture far from their animal heritage. Still, they are prime examples of possible combinations of animal traits, as well as exaggeration of an extrapolation upon those traits.

When making a composite animal, study the traits of each animal you want to include in the mix. It's just like any other set of correspondences–for an animal to protect your front door, try combining the loyal, brave dog with the focused, quick-striking snake. Or for a messenger of sorts, take the swift-footed cheetah and add the wings of a peregrine falcon to increase the possible avenues of travel. In any case, the goal is to combine the best features of each animal involved in order to create the necessary participant in the magic at hand. Some may turn out looking rather strange, but a lot of that is due to their novelty. As with any created servitor, experiment to find what works best.

A less extreme exercise is creating a variant on an existing animal. Cerberus, the three-headed dog who guards Hades, is a prime example. Oversized animals like Fenris also run rampant through story and lore. Animals of abundance, such as cattle, sheep and chickens, may be altered so that they are more productive in some capacity—not necessarily their species' original role in human domestication. Think of the possible magical uses, for instance, of the sheep that produced Jason's golden fleece, depending on what qualities you wish the fleece to carry.

The concept is simple—take a mundane species and alter either its size, number of certain appendages, color, or so on, to create an animal capable of performing whatever magical task is needed. It's usually less extreme than creating a composite animal but the effects are similar. It also eliminates the possible issue with combining animal traits that end up not being complementary.

I decided to experiment with this concept, so I made a new composite species of animal through servitor-forms. I opted to combine traits of grey wolves and red-tailed hawks to basically make wolves with wings—efficient predators in both the air and on land, the two elements I have the most daily contact with.

I gave them the social structure of wolves, with me as their alpha, but with an added bit of independence from the hawk. I also gave them the hawk's excellent eyesight. I designed them with a wolf's body, but with two wings sprouting from the shoulders. I made them entirely asexual and therefore nonreproducing and programmed them to feed on ambient energy, though if they needed to hunt I told them to be as wolves and seek the weak and infirm.

I created their physical anchors out of air-drying clay and placed a small bit of wolf fur and faux hawk feather in each one's belly. I periodically breathed energy into them to get a good buildup along with the energy of creation itself. I then invoked both Wolf and Hawk into me to pass their blessings on to the new species. I wrapped a strand of my hair around the head of each and gave them my final breath of life. I gave them their task as protectors of me, body, mind and soul, unless I set them to a different task. If they completed this latter task their default was to automatically return to me. I made them immortal, unless their physical forms were deliberately destroyed, or if they gained enough strength to become independent entities.

So somewhere on the astral plane there's now a pack of four winged wolves that'll cause a hell of a lot of trouble if anyone tries to harm me.

With this ritual I not only tested out the idea of creating a new composite species—which, let me tell you, is a definite

113

rush–but also the further utilization of animal parts in enhancing the composite traits. The fur and feathers definitely added a distinct strength to the animals; there was a decided enhancement of energy when I placed the items in their bellies.

I also found, as with so many other rituals of mine, that I internalized the energy. As I completed the creation process I astrally shifted to the form of one of the winged wolves. It is now a permanent part of my Self.

Do keep in mind that once a composite species gains a little self-awareness it will develop traits entirely independent of its parent species. The unicorn, for example, is quite more than simply a mixture of horse, deer and goat traits. You can program these habits and behaviors into the magical DNA of the species, or you can simply allow the animals to evolve on their own.

New Species

A more advanced variation is the creation of an entirely new species. Obviously there's a lot of leeway here–not only can a magician experiment within the confines of known fauna, but beings resembling nothing native to this plane may also be brought into an existence of sorts.

Oddly enough, there's a definite dearth of wholly unique species in traditional mythology and folklore. Most of what you'll find there is either a variation on an existing animal, or a composite animal. Only recently have writers and artists really begun exploring the realms of the new animal.

Some of the creatures found in the realms of cryptozoology–regardless of whether they're native to the physical plane or another–are quite obviously unlike any other species that we know of. Mothman and El Chupacabra, two of the better-known denizens of this area of study, aren't even remotely like anything familiar to us. Whether they've actually been sighted or simply began as local legend doesn't affect the fact that over the years they've accumulated their own notoriety and an energy that can certainly be put to use by the adventurous magician.

The art of species creation is an increasingly common theme in pop culture, particularly that infatuated with anime and manga. *Pokemon*, for instance, is based around a number of animals that, while they may resemble familiar species, are most certainly their own entities. Not only do they have their particular, often elementally derived, attributes, but they are capable of growth and maturation cycles; this can be adapted in your own workings as a growth pattern based on time or any other scale you invent. Pokemon have also been designed to be tamable and trainable, though some effort has to be put into the process, just as with physical animals. Each species has its own strengths and weaknesses, both mundanely and in the magical system that's been designed in their world.

Fantasy and sci-fi writers are particularly good inspiration. The Dark Ones from Barbara Hambly's *The Time of the Dark*, Terry Brooks' Machine-Beasts from the *Shannara* novels, the Shrowks in *A Voyage to Arcturus* by David Lindsay and the Alzabo from Gene Wolfe's *The Sword of the Lictor* are all examples of animals that, while possessing occasional traits reminiscent of terrestrial beasts, are unique species created wholly from the authors' minds (Barlowe's Guide to Fantasy — 1996/*Barlowe*/p. 2, 26, 58, 78). Of course, the *Star Wars* mythos has also given us a wide variety of creatures from creative minds. Stepping back a few decades there are beings in H.P. Lovecraft's world that were never spawned in our existence.

Movies in these genres have also spawned a number of unique species. The *Alien* and *Predator* series are obvious choices–in fact, just about any good sci-fi movie will have at least a couple of odd species bouncing about. And anyone who's seen *The Dark Crystal*, with the Skeksis and the urRu and all sorts of other fascinating beings, will know exactly what I'm going for here.

Yes, fantasy and sci-fi aren't based in our reality. But the entities that arise from their stories are just as viable as those who have been around for centuries. After all, classic mythologies served many of the same purposes for their respective cultures that modern-day stories do in ours–they teach lessons and cultural morals, they demonstrate acceptable and unacceptable personality characteristics, they record contemporary issues that become history and they simply entertain. Many of the archetypes discussed in mythology by the likes of Joseph Campbell can be found in today's storytelling, the *Star Wars* mythos being one of the finest examples. Try evoking an animal native to that terrain and see what sort of results you get–the initial communication may be a bit alien, for obvious reasons, but once all parties understand each other, the results are the same as with native species.

Designing Your New Animal

Again, it's best to start with a list of the desired traits and any magical acts the creation is expected to perform or aid with. Some things to keep in mind are:

–How does the animal move?

–How large is the animal?

–What is the basic structure of the animal–biped, quadruped, or something completely different?

–Is the animal carnivorous, herbivorous, omnivorous, or does it subsist on something entirely different? Remember, these don't have to stay along strict terrestrial biological lines–it's entirely possible to create an animal that feeds on rocks, or air, or even thoughts.

–How does it interact (at least in theory) with other animals, wild, domestic and/or fantastic, as well as with the human animal? What sort of communication does it use, i.e. body language, vocalizations, etc.? Can it communicate reasonably with other species?

–What survival traits has the animal developed, such as coat patterns, defensive structures like antlers or horns or something entirely disturbing like the sea cucumber's entrail vomiting?

–What is the species' social structure like? Is it solitary or gregarious? Does it vary from season to season? Is it territorial?

–What sort of habitat does it reside in?

–How long does it live in its natural environment?

–Is it related to any known species? Did it evolve from another species?

–How does it reproduce? Live birth? Eggs? Asexual reproduction (to include the possibility of an entirely neuter species)? Lighting itself on fire and then rising from the ashes?

–Does it have a lifespan?

–Is it wild or inherently domesticated? If wild, how difficult is it to tame/train/befriend/etc.?

Basically the key is to create a natural history of the species so that there are observable traits to draw from and use in magic. Created animals may even develop totemic traits over time as more energy is put into their existence–that is, they may end up with an archetypal energy that represents the species as a whole.

You may want to add magical attributes to the animal as well. The sky's the limit here.

–What element(s) is/are the animal associated with?

–Is the animal capable of human speech?

–Can the animal move faster or exist in harsher conditions than mundane animals or humans?

–Is the animal immortal? Is it impervious to certain conditions or injuries?

–What properties do the various body parts of the animal possess? Can it regrow missing parts?

–Can the animal perform any magical acts on its own? Is it sentient in a human manner, or another manner and if in another manner, how so?

Putting the Composite/New Species To Use

Once the natural and magical histories have been established, create a model or picture of the new animal. You can draw or paint a picture of the animal (which includes digital imagery), sculpt it out of clay or stone, or utilize pretty much any other visual medium. The more detail that can be put into it, the better. If you aren't much of an artist, have someone who is create it for you, or simply do the best you can do. Or write out a detailed encyclopedia essay about the animal. You might even try sigilizing the name and primary characteristics of the creature. Specifically with composites, there's also the possibility of using parts from the various physical animals that inspire the new creation as a base for your work. Refer to Chapter 6 on how to work with animal parts.

The representation need not be a masterpiece if it has the whole of your intent behind it. What matters is that it is an effective base for the energies you are bringing together and that it satisfactorily represents the new species to you, the creator.

Next, give the new animal life through a ritual. Formally name it and perhaps recite a story or account of the animal's attributes. Then charge the objectified animal as you will. Use the statue/drawing/etc. as a focus for future magical acts. Feed it regularly if it requires nourishment, give it attention if it is particularly social, and allow it to claim territory if that is its preference.

One possibility in magical use is that of a reproducing species. If a certain task is programmed into the species, as with any servitor, then if the species replicates there will be that many more individual entities working towards the task. Insect-type creations are particularly adept at this, as such animals reproduce by the thousands.

It's also recommended that a method of total elimination of the new animal also be created; every species should have a weak spot. It's not absolutely necessary to use this failsafe, but if the species you create can reproduce independently it may be a good idea to prevent overpopulation–after all, the animals are an extension of you, and you must control your magic, not the other way around. Another option is to create a certain number of individuals and design the mortality rate to be higher than the birth rate to the point that the species eventually dies out on its own. Or you can make a 1:1 birth-death ratio inherent.

I suppose if you're incredibly attached to your new species you can treat it like the virtual pets that have become popular in recent years. Make gifts of the animals to friends, study and develop the species over time–other magical practitioners may find them quite useful in their own rituals, and may even create and/or discover new traits. After all, this is how just about every mythological being has gained hir power, through the continued attention of human beings. Just be aware of what it is you are creating, and don't allow it to become a liability instead of an asset.

Sigilonodon

One of my first experiments in creating a new species was a joint effort with Taylor Ellwood. After a scrapped idea or two we came up with an idea for a creature that could capture energy for a purpose. We started with a basic lizard type animal, about seven or eight inches long, which is native to the astral plane. Its purpose was to capture ambient energy within a specific territory set by the magician, collect it and then use it to charge a sigil.

The lizard–dubbed sigilonodon–had a number of adaptations designed to aid in this process. The most notable were a pair of very flexible membranes stretched along the sides of the body between the front and back legs. These membranes were capable of extending up to a full body-length in front of the animal to grasp the energy. Three separate excretions caused the energy to stick to the membranes, release the energy if necessary, and digest it into a pure form; the purified energy was then absorbed through the skin and stored in the body. The sigilonodon was designed to only require a small amount of energy itself for sustenance, but could store almost limitless quantities within itself.

On its shoulders was a large scale. If a sigil was transferred to this scale, the animal immediately released all contained energy into charging it and then shifted all efforts beyond self-survival to continuing to charge the sigil. This went on until the sigil's intent was successfully completed, at which point the mating instinct kicked in. Since sigilonodons were hermaphroditic egg-layers, each would lay its own clutch of eggs to be fertilized by the other; then both adults would die. Three days later the eggs all hatched, and out of each one only one young survived, having killed its siblings; thus a 1:1 population rate. The new sigilonodon then returned to its parent's territory to start the process anew.

Using Animal Characteristics In Other Entities

Sometimes it's preferable to just add a certain animal characteristic to another type of entity. Say, for instance, that you're creating your own view of the Divine–a personal pantheon. Rather than simply having animals that are associated with each deity, you want them to possess characteristics of that animal, which usually heightens the bond between deity and animal as it internalizes the animal energy.

Refer to totemism for getting ideas (see Chapter 1). If you want to create a water-based huntress deity, you have plenty of options–but keep in mind that each of these options has hir own particular quirks. For instance, giving her qualities of a dolphin will probably make her much more intelligent and even-tempered than if she was a shark deity. A moray eel goddess would be a lot less social than an orca deity. And a seal or sea lion entity would have the advantage of being native to both water and land.

In addition, think about how you want the animal essence to manifest. With our aforementioned water goddess, you could give her the lower body of the dolphin for swift swimming. A more war-prone divinity may have the head of a crocodile and the body of a strongly built human.

Animal Parts as Entity Bases

It's common to use a physical base when creating any sort of entity, and animal remains are just as suitable as anything. It's particularly useful when you want to impart your servitor with qualities from that particular animal; you can also combine parts for physical bases for astral composite animals.

Remember that successful work with animal parts does require some respect and ability to work with the residual energy of the animal that once wore the body. First off, you'll want to get permission from that energy from each component. Otherwise the feathers, fur and other bits may not cooperate properly with the base you're creating, and it's their energy that helps give an extra bond to the animal traits you're imbuing your species with. You can certainly forgo animal parts in your base, but having the pure influences of the animals who inspired your species there helps create a bond to the parent species.

Sometimes it's not possible to have access to certain animal parts, especially those that are illegal to possess or otherwise difficult to obtain. My winged wolves had real wolf fur in them, but I had to use imitation hawk feathers. In fact, if you want to do a vegan version you can even use fake fur, plastic claws and teeth, and so on. You might try dedicating these faux bits to the species they represent. Evoke the totem of the species, present the parts to them with your statement of intent, and ask hir to place the species' energy into the fake pieces.

Chapter 5
Shapeshifting

Shapeshifting is quite possibly one of the most alluring forms of animal magic. Mythology and folklore are full of tales of humans who shift into animal form, whether by will or by curse, of animals that become human to woo a man or woman, and of early creation myths where the physical reality was much more malleable and all beings could shift their forms as they pleased.

Shapeshifting may be divided roughly into two categories–therianthropic and nontherianthropic. Therianthropy is a condition/state of mind/etc. in which a person believes hirself to be, in spirit, a certain type of animal. I set that section apart because of the intimacy of the bond between human and animal, and because the nature of the theory and practice behind it varies somewhat from other forms of shapeshifting.

Non-therian shifting

Shapeshifting is a form of invocation in which the magician allows the animal consciousness to take at least partial control of the body. It is a truly unique experience, an exchange that allows the animal spirit to wear flesh again, and give the human a chance to see what it is, for a brief time, to truly be that animal. Invocation may be performed with any level of totem animal.

During the Inquisition the rural lore that witches could change themselves or others into animals became a fairly prevalent accusation/confession. The idea is much older; the Romans told tales of: "the *strix*...a woman by day but at night flies [as an owl] on amorous, murderous or cannibalistic errands." (Witches of the Atlantic World — 2000/*Cohn*/p. 117) Shapeshifting, particularly by shamans, is still a part of the lore of certain indigenous tribes; these shapeshifters may be benevolent or, as in the case of the skinwalker of the Southwest United States, malevolent. Sometimes a malevolent shapeshifter such as the werewolf is seen in a sympathetic light; in the 1150s Marie de France composed a *lai* entitled *Bisclavret* in which a male werewolf's unfaithful wife takes advantage of his condition.

Classic lycanthropy often involved either performing a ritual of invocation of an animal spirit or contact–sometimes unwanted–with an otherworldly entity. This process often made use of a belt or other item made from the skin of the animal the magician wished to become, many times in tandem with hallucinogenic drugs. A famous Russian spell involves driving a copper knife into a tree stump and pacing round it while chanting a certain set of lines.

Lycanthropy was sometimes a curse rather than a

blessing. A Danish tale, like *Bisclavret*, involved a young husband who accidentally revealed his inherited condition to his wife. Unlike the hapless French werewolf, this one gave his wife the key to releasing him from the monthly plight. As he, in wolf form, ran towards her on a full moonlit night, "she ripped off her apron, then struck the wolf in the face with the cloth" (Deer dancer - 1995/*Jamal*/p. 161). This removes the curse from him once and for all, though no explanation is expressly given as to how. It's similar to other stories in which true love supposedly solves everything, an exaggeration of the effects of that buoyant feeling.

Sometimes the curse was cast upon an offending mortal. Lycaeon, King of Arcadia, attempted to covertly serve human flesh to several of the Olympian deities. Incensed, they caused him and his sons to be changed into wolves; in fact it is from the king's name that we get the word "lycanthropy." Some sources also say that their descendants would live as wolves one year out of seven, or for a seven-year period. This mythos pops up at intervals in various European folk tales.

The physical shift is an iffy proposition for magicians. Some believe it is possible, while others claim we are too entrenched in stagnant physical reality to be able to change our bodies that dramatically. Indeed, the necessary changes to the human biology in such a short period of time, were they to occur, would seemingly cause instant death. There are those who argue that such a powerful magical act has built-in failsafes, though none have stepped forward with definite proof (given modern human tendencies to figuratively and literally dissect anything new and different, it may not be such a bad idea to keep one's mouth shut in the event of possessing such knowledge).

Nonphysical shifts are wholly available to the magic-user. In speaking of an earlier time when animals and humans were supposedly able to switch forms with ease, Michael Harner comments, "While the mythical animal-human unity is lost in ordinary reality, it still remains accessible in nonordinary reality...in the altered state of consciousness, the mythical past is immediately accessible" (The Way of the Shaman — 1990/Harner/p. 57-58).

Wearing costumery and mimicking the movements of the chosen animal in ritual help to alter the consciousness sufficiently to allow the energy of that animal into the magician's system. Alternately, a guided meditation leading to astral or inner projection, depending on whether you believe the consciousness goes within or without, can lead to a very powerful sensate shift. Simply travel to the astral and allow the form you use to change shape. Will your astral form to become that of the animal in question, asking for aid from a totem if so desired. Explore the experience in detail, imprinting as much of the memory of the experience as possible upon your mind for future use.

Once a mental shift can be attained at short notice the

ability to change one's consciousness can be invaluable. I have invoked Wolf and Cougar in times when I was threatened physically, Cat to increase sexual allure and Horse to give me the strength and resolve to complete physically laborious tasks. Need mental or visual focus? Call Hawk's energy into yourself. Want to project gentleness without seeming weak? Bring Deer's influence into play.

Invoking a primary totem animal is the easiest way to initiate a shift, though secondary and tertiary animals will also be effective–a lot depends on how much work the practitioner has done with a specific animal. Nontotemic animals, such as fantastic creatures or extinct species, may also be involved in shapeshifting.

Dance is an incredibly powerful tool in invocative shapeshifting. The excitatory nature of the trance helps to touch more primal areas of the brain, triggering an easier conception of the animal mindset. The more deep into trance the dancer goes into, the more animal traits will appear. Senses that in a human are usually sort of ignored, such as smell, may be not so much enhanced as noticed more. The motion will become more like that of the animal, and the dancer may begin to make noises of the creature s/he is shifting into. The mental process becomes less human and becomes more an animal observing through human eyes.

One tool that I've found particularly effective is costumery. I have been dancing in a full timber wolf skin since

2002, and have since then created other costumes from other skins. One benefit of dancing in a skin is that the spiritual residue leftover from when the animal dies often enhances a shapeshifting experience–the spirit enjoys having a body to ride again but also contributes hir own sense-memories to the magician's shift. Putting on the skin of the animal being shifted to is also a very powerful psychological trigger; it is symbolic of becoming that animal, which is why so many paleopagan cultures utilized skins in rituals. It is a powerful form of sympathetic magic and can be mutually beneficial. If you wish to read up on working with animal parts more check out Chapter 6.

It is recommended that only one animal be danced per ritual (on an individual basis.) If a magician tries to switch from one to another in the same trance the second shift may not work nearly as well–it's better to focus on only one and get a stronger connection then to break up concentration at the height of ecstasy. Also, if more than one person will be invoking in the same ritual, be aware of any species conflicts. While most magicians should have enough self-control to prevent themselves from being ridden by the animal they call on it doesn't help to tempt fate by having, say, Owl and Mouse in the same circle. Chances are nothing will happen, but if the Owl person is a bit unstable or lacks control s/he may use the shapeshift as an excuse to be incredibly stupid, and possibly harmful.

Therianthropy[1]

"*In a totemistically conceived society the various clans or groups are regarded as having semi-animal, semi-human ancestors, from which the animal species of like name is likewise descended; and the members of the clan are prohibited both from killing and eating the beasts who are their cousins and from marrying within their totem group.*"

—Joseph Campbell, *Primitive Mythology*

While many shapeshifters gain their ability to change from an external source there are those whose animal side is inherent. Stories of such people tend to be more common in cultures where having a connection with an animal was seen favorably, as opposed to more conservative societies where such a condition was viewed as a sure sign of evil.

Today's "born" shapeshifters often fall into the category of therianthropy (from the Greek *therios*, "beast" and *anthropos*, "man") (http://www.shifters.org —May 2005/*Jakkal*). A therianthrope is a person who has an incredibly strong bond

---

[1] The vast majority of the information in this section comes from two sources. The primary source is the internet, specifically http://www.shifters.org and conversation at http://forums.therianthropy.org. A secondary source is Rosalyn Greene's The Magic of Shapeshifting. I encountered the book first, purchasing and reading it cover to cover, then discovered the online resources a couple of months later. According to certain therian folk active in the internet community, Ms. Greene blatantly stole information from shifters.org without giving credit; check out some of the reviews at http://www.amazon.com or search forums.therianthropy.org for her name to find the occasional discussion on this subject. Conversely, in her book the author states that "the portion of the shifter movement that exists on the Internet is very badly organized, has a dubious reputation, and is, sadly, often a 'fishing ground' for all sorts of strange cults." (p. 226) Go figure. As always, I urge you to make your own decision in regards to this particular debate.

with a particular species or, as in the case of a cladotherian, an entire genus or family of animal, to the point where s/he identifies as the animal in some manner beyond a regular totemic bond. A few therianthropes claim bonds with more than one divergent species of animal, such as wolf and panther.

Theories abound as to the source of this connection. Past lives as animals or being an animal soul in a human body are two of the more common ones, both of which require a bit of a leap of faith for those not entirely convinced of species-specific souls or reincarnation. Strong totemic bonds are also cited as possible causes of therianthropy and, of course, purely psychological explanations range from early childhood imprinting to animal personification of the more primitive sections of the brain.

It's not agreed-upon whether or not therianthropy is magical in nature. Some therians are also magicians, but a number don't work with any esoterica whatsoever. A lot depends on your definition of magic. For instance, if you believe it to be a supernatural thing, but you view therianthropy as natural, the two are in opposition. On the other hand there's always Aleister Crowley's definition, "Magick [sic] is the Science and Art of causing Change to occur in conformity with Will" (Magick Without Tears — 1994/Crowley/p. 26). In that case therianthropic shapeshifting as an act of Will is as magical as any spell or ritual.

There is, of course, the option that every single one of

us is stark raving mad, but I tend to keep that one on the back burner for just about everything I do. After all, humans worldwide have exhibited numerous behaviors that could be classified as insane—extreme hostility towards other humans, other species, and the self. Anyone who has passively observed *Homo sapiens* in a tightly packed living arrangement for any length of time will soon begin to question just why these animals are putting themselves through such torture. And the constriction placed upon anyone who works a regular job, if seen from the point of view of your everyday dog, is such an exercise in self-destruction that it's a wonder anyone willingly participates in it.

I personally identify as a therianthrope (wolf, of course), because it benefits me to do so on several levels. I tend towards a combination of the totemic, imprinting and personification theories because that is what explains my identification with *Canis lupus* most convincingly. The totemic aspect allows me to work with not only my primary totem, Wolf, much more easily, but the wild nature also allows me to work with other totems on a more sympathetic level. The imprinting gives me a clue in detangling my own internal wiring when I do metamorphic work for the purpose of exploring and reprogramming myself. And the personification works with both of these, because it allows me to understand the more bestial aspects of human nature, as well as identify when those aspects are ascendant in my behavior, and to claim them as my own instead of being a separate entity.

It also explains personality quirks that arose as I grew older. I've always thought of myself as a wolf to some degree or another, ever since my first exposure to that particular energy early on. Because I lived rather isolated from my childhood friends, I had a lot of time to myself, and spent a lot of it trying my damnedest to be a wolf. I was crepuscular (most active at dusk and dawn), fascinated with the chase and occasional capture of the rabbits and other wild animals near my home and was constantly running off into the woods where I felt most comfortable. When I first read Jack London's *White Fang* around the age of seven I strongly identified with the title character, a semiferal wolf-dog hybrid. And when my friends and I would play make-believe games I was always, regardless of setting, a wolf. They eventually got used to it and just found ways to work me into the strangest stories.

All these early behaviors imprinted heavily, and the part of me that I thought of as lupine never went away, even as I became more enmeshed in human society with as I grew older. There were times I actually tried exorcising the wolf because I thought my more animal behaviors were signs of insanity, but to no avail. I found, through practice, that embracing the wolf is a lot healthier and useful than denying that part of me.

The wolf self has actually become integrated enough into my being that I'm in a near-constant state of phantom shift; in other words, my energetic body is the shape of a wolf that wraps around my physical human form. I commonly experience phantom ears, tail, muzzle and paws, and less frequently the entire body superimposed over my flesh. When I look at myself as wolf, I see a small, rather scrawny wolf-bitch with a dirty white pelt and amber eyes. During more intense mental/emotional/spiritual shapeshifts, observers have "seen" this form in their mind's eye. I've also been able to consistently record a change in eye color (from blue to amber, though not always throughout the entire iris) and occasionally my canines will lengthen and sharpen noticably, though not dramatically. On the other hand, these physical changes could be attributed to subconscious wishful thinking or shifts in perception on the part of all involved—Occam's Razor once again!

Whether my wolf is a product of my imagination, a characterization of universal mammalian territorial and social behaviors or a result of a strong totemic bond, the fact remains that it is a part of me as much as anything else. Identifying as a therianthrope allows me to satisfy the human need to label things, and gives me a basic structure and a rather loose community to work with to develop myself further.

Regardless of background, most therians identify as being an animal in some form at all times. Unlike furry fandom, therianthropy A) focuses on "real" animals as opposed to anthropomorphics (human/animal crosses—everything from Bugs Bunny to the werewolves from "The Howling") and B) is a constant part of the person, rather than a roleplaying game.

While there is some crossover between furries and therians, they should not be considered one and the same or subgroups of each other (keep in mind that I'm speaking generally about both groups; as always there will be numerous exceptions to every rule–in fact, think of these as guidelines rather than rules).

Therians also exhibit the entire range of behavior of their phenotype (the species they identify with), not just the aggressive ones. Even therians who have no contact with physical members of their phenotype seem to have a strong behavioral resemblance. Some debate that this could be because they have a tendency to study the animals and thereby internalize what they learn, whether consciously or unconsciously. In defense of therians, books often can take the place of the parent/social group a young animal has naturally, and so this is how the animal side of the therian learns the "how-tos" of existence.

You can tell some newbies by their loud talk of bloodlust, meat cravings and the ever-present need to howl at the moon. Sometimes this is the only way they know how to express their animal side and they grow to become comfortable with their entire animal self. Other times, though, it can be a sign of someone who's been playing too many White Wolf LARPs. (Of course, that argument could be made by debunkers in regards to just about everyone who practices magic, claims an Other side, or is otherwise involved in metaphysics.) Time separates the pups from the pack, so to speak, and those who are just in it to be trendy or "special" eventually find another fad to chase.

I, and some other therians, strive for balance of their human and animal sides, though there are a few who wish to destroy one or the other. Greene, in fact, makes some suggestions as to how to "cure" therianthropy, some based along old traditions regarding lycanthropy, and others being reversals of her tips on increasing the therianthropic influence (The Magic of Shapeshifting — 2000/*Greene*/p. 221-224). Some therians experience species dysphoria, the ever-present feeling that one has been born into the body of the wrong animal. These sometimes exhibit a strong loathing for the actions of humans–and who can blame them, given humanity's treatment of nature, animals included?

Unlike the clinical lycanthrope a therianthrope does not go uncontrollably feral at the full moon. There are those who are affected by lunar legends, whether consciously or subconsciously, and who do experience stronger energy from their animal side when the moon is full, though anyone who's worked in an emergency room will tell you that "odd" behavior in general tends to rise during the full moon. Lunar light can be a good psychological/magical tool in working with therian energy, and makes a nice nightlight for nocturnal ramblings.

Though shifting can occur unexpectedly it can also be deliberately incited. I have found that by reading about wolves or werewolves, by a spending couple of hours by myself out in the woods or simply by concentrating on my lupine aspect I can bring on a decent mental shift. If I want to vividly bring out the Wolf I'll do a full invocation, with or without my wolfskin, around a fire circle with the drums going full speed. Or I'll visualize my phantom wolf form.

Sometimes my Wolf just shows up on her own. Often this is when I haven't been giving her enough exercise. I usually try to keep a decent balance of Wolf and Human at all times, but being in a human body forces me to put more effort towards human concerns. Heavy emotions, especially those that provoke more primal fight-or-flight reactions, will cause her to rise to the surface. If I haven't eaten in a while and my blood sugar drops, my attention focuses fully on the hunt and downing of large quantities of food—while generally I can attribute cravings for meat to protein and fat deficiencies, my Wolf does make a strong bid in that direction a good bit of the time. She tends to remind me of the more basic needs of my body, and gets distressed if I neglect them.

Putting the Wolf back to sleep is relatively simple. If I want a quiet method, I simply concentrate on something else, something utterly human. If the shift is a more insistent one I'll either go for a walk or, if space and company permit, go for a run through the nearest patch of park or woodland. In the event that I can't do either, I can always dance myself to exhaustion in my ritual room. In short, the shift can be treated similarly to any other invocation. Persistent dampening of the animal side does lead to long-term problems, the same as any other suppression of personality.

Speaking of shifting, how about those legends of the physical shift that persist even today? Opinions vary within the therian community. Some folks believe it is simply symbolic, while others believe it to be a distinct possibility. A few even experiment regularly with methods of attaining this elusive state. For the most part, therians tend to experience shifts on nonphysical levels such as astral, dream, mental and etheric planes. Some tend to stick to one or two types of shift, while others go through numerous types, sometimes even simultaneously.

Therianthropy, Otherkin, and Aspecting

Therianthropy is sometimes included under the heading of Otherkin. Otherkin are those who believe that part of their being is nonhuman. Again, as with therianthropy specifically, the Otherkin community tends to have several theories as to the source of their other-ness. The most popular by far is reincarnation, though some insist that somewhere a few generations removed a nonhuman entity literally mated with a human ancestor. Many claim highly detailed memories of lives on alternate planes of reality, whether Earthly or otherwise. While most people who claim the title of Otherkin express humanoid nonhuman sides (elves and dragons seem to be particularly common) therians usually have mundane animals as their nonhuman aspects. The "Other-by-blood" theory also isn't nearly as prevalent among therians, though there are numerous stories in indigenous cultures of how certain families were literally descended from an animal.

Obviously this can be a difficult concept to swallow. Start with the general opinion that these people are probably at least a little imbalanced. Add in the folks who do their utmost to fulfill that prophecy by being as outlandish as possible, and occasionally even wandering about with untreated genuine mental disorders. Toss in the human tendency to alienate and degrade those who are different, and you have a recipe for disaster on many occasions.

On the other hand, there's also the theory that regardless of whether these personality aspects are in their nature microcosmic, macrocosmic or both, that they are a part of the people who claim them. In other words, it doesn't matter whether a given Otherkin claimant is an overzealous Tolkien fan or a reincarnated being from one of the many planes of reality that exist in this Universe who somehow managed to manifest here. If they're not causing any harm, who really cares? And if they can create effective magic out of it, so much the better!

Actually, deliberate personality aspecting in general can be an exceptionally useful tool for metamorphic magic. Most magicians possess a wide variety of personality traits, and often these can be in direct conflict with each other. This sometimes leads to behaviors that seem contradictory and confusing. Personality aspecting may be used as a tool for better understanding groupings of these traits.

I spent one summer living as four different personae. I had observed an increasing tendency to react to a single incident in two, three and occasionally four different ways at once, all with equal vehemence. This, of course, confused the hell out of me. We tend to identify as one persona (usually the ego) and think of ourselves in terms of "I am this, but I am not this, this or this."

I had talked with my friend Nicholas Graham about the different Selves and read about invoking these Selves in Peter J. Carroll's writing (Liber Null and Psychonaut — 1987/*Carroll*/p. 41-44). Rather than using the eight colors of magic found in standard Chaos texts, I combined bits and parts of Robert Anton Wilson's writings on the first two psychological circuits (Prometheus Rising — 1983/*Wilson*/p. 25-70) with totemic qualities and an expansion of my own therianthropy.

I divided my various traits and behaviors into four distinct personae. Lupa, my primary persona at the time, was Friendly Weakness–a female wolf sort of person and the typical pacifist hippie. Lupus, her brother, was a sullen teenage goth boy given to complaining, a short fuse and general mayhem; he took up the place of Hostile Weakness. Hostile Strength was personified by Cougar, a persona who only came out when needed for defense and intimidation. Friendly Strength became a Cat, sexual and personable and quite confident.

I created a separate wardrobe for each of these, then proceeded to become each one in turn for a day or two at a time. As the weeks progressed I found myself becoming more familiar with each and being able to invoke each one as necessary without the need of a ritual. After about six weeks I spent a four-day period being separate personae for the last time, then reunited all my traits into one being who was, and still is, all four of these at once in various proportions.

I'm going to take a moment to apologize to the more traditional section of the therian community (if a decade or so can be considered tradition). I realize that conventional wisdom in regards to therianthropy dictates that therianthropy is not created—it simply *is* a part of the person. I've run into the attitude that the definition of therianthropy should remain pure, that after a certain amount of deviation from the standard definition the term therianthropy no longer applies and another ought to be used.

While I certainly respect this viewpoint I am approaching therianthropy both as a therian and an experimental magician. From the one perspective yes, I believe that therianthropy is an inherent thing, that I am as much Wolf as I am Human. The other viewpoint, though, calls for speculation and extrapolating on theories. After all, nobody's quite sure what the cause of therianthropy is, be it past lives, strong totemic bonds, or personifications of certain parts of the psyche.

In addition, the experiment I ran affected not only my human side but my lupine therian side as well, and so I found it worth mentioning in speaking of therianthropy and magic. My initial intent had nothing to do with my therian nature; in fact, I expected the temporary schism to only affect my humanity. What I am describing here is a unique situation that occurred on all levels of my being as a result of my experimentation and should not be interpreted as being a standard part of what is accepted as therianthropy. In fact, I've yet to speak to another therianthrope who has undertaken this deliberate personality aspecting.

So, disclaimers aside, allow me to delve further into this querying. In the aforementioned experiment each of my four aspects (which were all parts of one personality, not separate personalities in and of themselves) had hir own therian identity—that is, a part of hirself that was distinctly not human and that went beyond a totemic bond. I judge this not by how long I was aware of the animals' presences in my existence, but how strong the bond was. Each aspect was equally human and animal. Lupa and Lupus were as much Wolf as Human, and Cougar and Cat were just as feline as hominid. The human and animal parts of each were subaspects. When I reintegrated all my aspects, however, my therian side once again was simply Wolf.

On the other hand I know therian-type folk who consider their human and animal natures to be two separate personality aspects. I never have done so, but then again, there are still many uncertain topics in regards to therianthropy.

Whether or not you consider this to be true therianthropy is your own decision. I base it primarily on how strong and balanced the human and animal sides are. I also understand that the concept of personality aspecting can be too analytical and complicated for some folks who prefer to simply see things as a blend of what they are. For others it's too close to inviting schizophrenia. The reason for personality aspecting is to separate different groupings of traits for the purpose of understanding them better–it is tool just like anything else.

Furthermore, everyone's personality is widely malleable. We have within ourselves a full spectrum of emotions and psychological patterns; it is our background and experiences that shape which ones are active and which are dormant. Some speculate that every human is a therianthrope, but most never realize is–the animal traits go unrecognized for what they are. If this is true, then thrianthropy is only a matter of discovering and awakening those traits.

Let's suppose that, as with other personality aspects, it is possible to create one that is therian in nature–one that combines both human and animal traits (or souls, if you will) in a more or less equal balance. Bring in your totemic work to help create this persona if it is necessary or if it is a preexisting part of that set of traits. You can also work from a more psychological perspective by personifying the more primitive, instinctual parts of your psyche in animal form (a good example would be the first and second circuits in Leary's eight-circuit model). The stronger the bond with the animal is, the stronger the behavior traits will become. Remember that a therianthrope is someone who is as much the animal as the human (if not an animal in human skin), and that s/he more or less possesses all traits of both in balance. As you work with each persona, allow hir animal nature to be an equal part to the human aspects. Not only does this strengthen your ability to work with your therian nature, but it also increases flexibility when shifting from one focus to the next. In fact, any activity that involves shapeshifting breaks up blockages and removes stagnation.

In order to recreate my aspecting experiment for yourself–whether you are working with preexisting aspects or not–first gather traits that are complementary to each other into their own individual groups. Analyze each group and then begin to build a persona based on those traits. If it makes it easier, snag a character sheet from a roleplaying game and use it as a worksheet for this process–obviously some traits on the sheet, particularly the physical ones, won't be applicable. But the format can be used to organize your thoughts on each persona. Give each aspect a name, detail hir gender identification and sexuality (not necessarily the same as your own!), and perhaps even write up a brief explanation of what s/he is like. Since you're working with animal magic you may also consider deciding what animal each persona resembles the

most. It's best to limit the number of personae you work with–
four is a nicely balanced number, though two or three also work
well. If you're feeling ambitious, there's a great ritual based on
the eight colors of Chaos magic in *Konton* magazine 2.1 (Liber
Chromatria: An Exploration of the Eight Selves -
2005/*Ceilede*/p. 20-22).

Once you have made yourself familiar with your aspects,
it's time to bring them to life. Think of it as character acting–
be each persona to the greatest degree you can for a period of
time. In addition to acting the part, you may consider creating
a separate physical appearance and set of mannerisms for
each. You may switch personae on a daily, weekly or even
greater basis, or you may simply choose to invoke as is
appropriate to each situation you encounter. The more you
become each aspect the better you will understand the traits
inherent in each, and the more control you will have over your
own behavior as you can invoke or banish your individual selves
at will.

Keep in mind that these are all a part of you. It's best to
discontinue the experiment after a set amount of time–a
month or two at most for your first time through–to avoid
become permanently fragmented. Recognizing that you are
more than a single dimension is not the same as provoking
something akin to Multiple Personality Disorder within yourself.
Control and communication among your personae is vital–
even at the height of my aspecting I was still equally aware of

the activities of all my personae and found the inactive ones still communicating with each other and with whoever was "out" at the time. After all, they are all a part of me, and I am able to access all of my conscious self with equal ease.

This can be repeated at intervals; I personally find that once a year will suffice, and that summer is usually the best season for me to work. Try using a different manner of division each time. The four directions/elements/etc. division is a good starter, but you can also use anything from a Jekyll and Hyde dichotomy to the seven chakras/Personal Totem Pole model and beyond. This helps you understand yourself from different angles and prevents you from becoming stuck in a rut.

Finally, if you're interested in finding out more about aspecting, therianthropy and Otherkin in general I'm currently in the process of assembling a book on the subject.

Lupa

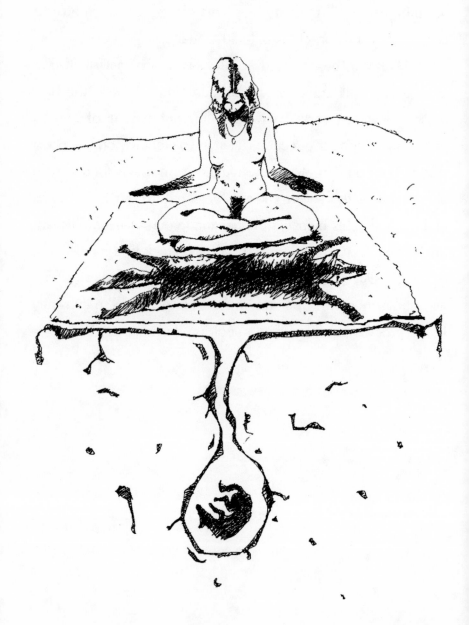

Chapter 6
Working With Animal Parts

The second most controversial topic in the field of animal magic is working with animal parts.[1] Magic workers vary in their support of animal welfare and animal rights. Some are avid hunters, others are full-fledged PETA members, and the majority has at least one pet sharing their domicile. This results in a wide variety of opinions on using animal parts in magic, ritual and everyday life. As with everything else in this book, it is your responsibility alone to create your own boundaries.

I've been creating ritual tools, jewelry and other artwork out of animal parts since around 1998 or so. I'd picked up the beadwork I'd learned in a high school art class when I was bored one winter break during college. The nearest place I could find beads in my rural area was a small town not too far from my home. There I found a family-owned shop that catered to the regional powwow circuit. Amid hundreds of beads and findings there were also leftover scraps from the fur industry, whole pelts, bones, feathers and plenty of other remains. I snagged a bag of deerskin scraps to make pouches to put my beadwork on, and that was where it all started.

[1] The most controversial, of course, is animal sacrifice, which will be discussed in the next chapter.

It's become a fairly major part of my practice–in a one-bedroom apartment I usually make the bedroom into my joint art and ritual room, and trust me–I need the space. A lot of my materials are secondhand–I've got old taxidermy mounts, used fur coats and stoles, bone beads from costume jewelry and other flea market items. I work with furs, leather, bones and other things because I want to give them a more dignified existence than being a trophy on some yahoo's wall or a "luxury" article worn by someone who's probably never seen the aftermath of the fur industry.

I can appreciate creative taxidermy–I've seen some mounts that were incredibly true to the animal's live form, that were obviously done with a nod to the natural beauty. On the other hand, I've seen things that made me sick. The worst, I believe, was a full-mount coyote forever frozen at the moment the trap snapped onto his foreleg, complete with horrified expression.

Now, I'm not one to stick my head in the sand. I know how horrific many animals' deaths are. They come into my hands every day with a story to tell. I've seen PETA's footage of fur farms, and I can only imagine what it must be like for a wild animal caught in a trap to sit and wait for hir death to arrive, or to be so desperate to escape that s/he chews hir own foot off.

This is why I support organizations that work for animal welfare, like the ASPCA, as well as those that work to preserve endangered species. The Defenders of Wildlife is my preferred nonprofit group, and a percentage of my financial income for this book goes to them.

I do go through personal moral quandaries from time to time over this issue. Every time I sit down and search the various options and consequences and my own thoughts and feelings. I always come up with the same answer in the end: Yes, I could stop working with animal parts the way I do, but it wouldn't stop the industry, and if I didn't create better forms for these parts, who would?

In addition, leather and fur and sometimes other parts are processed with harmful chemicals. Burying them in the Earth or burning them would release these chemicals in a concentrated and harmful manner. I've also asked some of the remains whether they'd like to simply be disposed of in some safer manner; for the most part they were severed from their lives abruptly, and they tend to want to stick around this plane a bit longer, and more often than not welcome the opportunities I offer them. It's gotten to the point where I've become sort of a dead-thing magnet—people who've gone flea marketing with me have noticed that I always seem to find the old coats and random pelts and things, and a couple have even noticed that it's a mutual attraction. Probably a lot of it is simply a trained eye, but there have been a few instances where I really had to hunt for something, while other times the article almost seemed to jump out at me. At one point, my friend (and guest essayist) Nicholas Graham and a former partner of his were able

153

to feel the interaction between me and a coyote skin I rescued from a pile of junk at one booth.

Finally, while my ceasing to work with animal parts would decrease the amount of demand by a tiny fraction I believe it doesn't balance out the benefits of what I do with them. Very few people work with remains the way I do, and my stopping my activities will not single-handedly put the slaughter of animals to a stop. Therefore until there are no longer remains to be worked with I will keep doing what I've been doing for years.

So yes, I am aware of the seemingly contradictory nature of my choices, and I do review them periodically to make sure I haven't lost my focus, and to adjust to any changes in philosophy and experiences that affect my standpoint. Others with the same practices would do well to take a step back and look at things honestly now and then, just to be sure.

Getting Started

First off, you're going to need to figure out exactly what your end product will be, and what components you'll need to create it. If you're working with someone else's formula or project directions chances are it'll call for specific components. Otherwise, keep in mind what exactly you'll be doing with the final product. Any creation involving water or long periods of time outdoors requires something waterproof, such as a tooth or bone (claws won't work, as the outer covering will soften and fall off.) Same goes for anything involving fire. Soft, stitchable items such as poppets will probably need fur or leather, as will pouches.

As for materials there's a wide variety available. Dried and tanned furs, leather, feathers, bones and skulls, teeth, claws and even innards make their way into magical creations on a regular basis. Most of these are derived either from fur farms which provide pelts for the fur coat industry, slaughterhouses that process meat for consumption by both humans and animals and to a lesser extent individual hunters and trappers. Very few people are willing to scavenge roadkill, though that can yield freebies with a little bit of work and a strong stomach, or the patience to wait until the meat rots and leaves bones behind. (Keep in mind, though, that many places have laws against picking up roadkill.)

It used to be that the only places one could reliably obtain animal parts was either through specialty leather shops or specific events like Native American powwows and SCA tourneys. With the public's aggressive command of the internet the options are much wider these days. Hundreds of stores sell all sorts of oddities from around the world. Online auction sites provide independent merchants with a wide audience of bidders. Type "craft fur" into any search engine and you'll find plenty of folks willing to provide you with what you're looking for. Of course, there's certainly something to be said of going through the experience of attending a powwow, pagan gathering or Renaissance festival, and most specialty shops are willing to look for specific items. In addition, some folks are like a friend of mine who's a leatherworker–he refuses to buy any leather without being able to handle it in person first.

You don't always have to buy unused items, either. Check any thrift store for previously worn fur and leather coats and purses, snakeskin vests and other items. Lurking at the local flea market may yield everything from hunter's leftovers to old taxidermy mounts. Costume jewelry is sometimes comprised of bone beads. Meat packing houses sometimes have discarded bones and hides, especially in areas where deer hunting is popular. Taxidermists occasionally have leavings available as well.

An important thing to keep in mind is legality. Many animal parts, particularly those of endangered or threatened species, are either restricted or completely illegal to own. Unlike some laws, those governing possession of animals, both alive and dead, are there for a good reason–namely, for the protection of scarce species. CITES (Convention on International Trade in Endangered Species of Wild Fauna and Flora) is a pact among many nations worldwide that was drafted in 1963 in order to control the trade of rare animals and plants.[3] Through this agreement as well as more local ordinances humans seek (with varying success) to prevent

---

[3] See http://www.cites.org for more information, including full text of CITES documents

certain species from reaching extinction. The moral of the story? Know where your purchase is coming from. Make sure there's documentation. If you know an animal has been killed illegally to obtain something, don't give the bastard who did the deed your money. Otherwise you're just perpetuating the cycle as well as putting yourself in danger of litigation. *Caveat emptor.*

Antiques are an exception. That leopard skin coat from the 1940's, for example, was made prior to the regulations that now protect the large cats of the world, and it's doubtful anyone's going to give you any trouble over it. So be on the lookout for old coats and stoles, rugs and taxidermy mounts.

A couple of warnings: all animal parts seem to be irresistible to domestic pets–there's pretty much no pet-proof option. Children are often enthusiastically attracted to animal parts (at least before they're taught the "Ewww, yuck!" reaction by their elders.) More often than not they're fascinated rather than repulsed by the wolfskin I wear when I dance. Keep this in mind when working with more delicate items. You might try giving curious children their own bits of fur and bone as a way of keeping them away from your own while making them quite delighted!

After a Successful Hunt

Once you've obtained what you need, it's time to do a bit of listening. I have found that after an animal dies there remains a residue attached to the body. It's similar to the psychic imprint that creates a haunt. It's not the soul or spirit, per se, but some level of consciousness stays attached to the body, some memory of the energy that once animated it. This bit of personality can be extremely helpful in the creation process.

The part of the body you're working with has an impact on how much of the residue is there. It seems to be stronger in parts that were used in communication while the animal was alive. The different parts of the body can be ordered roughly in how much they retain; the greatest is in the head, then the tail and legs, and finally the body, which primarily is used as a wrapper for the internal organs. The less processed something is, the stronger the impression. Fur is more "alive" than leather and natural feathers moreso than dyed ones. In addition whole pelts tend to be more active than partial ones. I try to avoid cutting up a pelt because it weakens the personality and the spirit within tends to not favor separation.

Most animals that end up dying at the hands of humans have pretty traumatic deaths. Face it—there's no way to make getting your throat cut or being gassed to death a fun experience. Animals simply do not understand why we kill them, even with something as relatively benign as intravenous euthanasia. This often leaves an incredibly negative taint to the remains that needs to be resolved before they can be integrated into magical work. One can use unpurified parts, of course, but I've always found that if a relationship is built between the practitioner and what is left of the spirit, the results of the magic are better as one can evoke that personality with more success and ease.

Parts that are acquired more naturally, such as molted feathers or shed fur, just don't have the intense energy of more violent acquisitions. There is a residue, but it's weaker and doesn't last as long. I've not found that, for example, using fur from a living dog in spellwork affects the dog—unless you intend it to. Still, such items can be quite useful in magic and for some carry a lot less guilt.

Any form of simple divination will work when communicating with the animal. Pendulum, coin toss, automatic writing and even direct intuitive conversation will work, though you'll certainly want to check your work to be sure you aren't just getting wishful thinking or random subconscious spoutings—especially if all you're getting is relative gibberish.

Ask the animal how s/he died, what you can do to help hir through and if s/he wants to be a part of your magic. Be patient. I have things I've held onto for years because they just couldn't seem to decide what they wanted to be next. Then do what you can to help it through the process of purification and subsequent magical work. Be sure, too, that the part is ready at that time–sometimes the bone or skin will want some time to rest or simply exist in your home.

If you intend to use parts from more than one animal in a project it's a good idea to check with them to make sure they're compatible. For instance I've played the part of Dr. Frankenstein by splicing a coyote face skin onto a wolf body when the latter was damaged and wanted completion, or replaced one tail with another by the animal's request. I ask both/all parts if they're amenable to the project, and if all is well I proceed with the "surgery".

Normally I don't have issues with mixing parts for other magical purposes, but it always helps to ask. I once got hold of a damaged deerskin wall hanging someone else made at a flea market. The centerpiece was a fox skull–and boy, was she pissed! One of her gripes was being placed on a shield with *chicken* feathers–a reminder: keep the whole predator/prey dynamic in mind! This was a rare instance, though; I've had very little issue with my own creations, though when I do I backtrack and make the necessary changes.

It's odd how the resonance of animal parts varies sometimes according to species. Whitetail deer seem to take death pretty well in stride. Wolves, foxes and other canids always seem to be incredibly relieved to find me. Cats tend to be graceful about the whole thing, though this doesn't mean they never get angry–they just have more finesse about it.

Birds always seem sad to have lost the ability to fly. Of course, there are always individual variations, but these are the general trends I've picked up. Try recording your results as you go along.

Purification and Energy Work

There are as many methods of purification as there are magical practitioners–and then some. The following is my personal S.O.P. when purifying animal parts.

First, take the piece and cleanse it with silver sage or a similar purificatory herb. I chose sage primarily because unlike water or salt it won't cause damage to more delicate things like fur or feathers, and because I like the smell and the energetic effect. Run it through the smoke until you feel it has been sufficiently purified.

As far as offerings go I have a number of small leather pouches, one for each animal whose remains I work with on a regular basis. Some, like deer, that I use frequently have a species-specific pouch; others, used less often, end up in combination pouches for a more general category, such as genus or family. For each piece I use I'll place anywhere from one to a dozen small drilled stones in the appropriate pouch. When the pouch is full I take these stones, make them into a necklace or pair of bracelets and give them to a person who works with that animal on some level, be it totemic or on a more physical level. It's a way of returning the energy to the species as a whole.

Rituals honoring the animal are also a good idea. Invoking either the individual spirit or the corresponding totem for a good dance or run in the woods works well, as does evocation for the purpose of inviting the spirit to a celebration in its honor. Animal spirits in general also seem to very much appreciate real-time aid to other critters, so volunteering at an animal shelter or making a donation to a nonprofit organization dedicating to helping wild or domestic animals will work as well.

When I am about to make an item out of a hide or other piece that needs cutting or stitching, I take the time to essentially put the residue to rest. Perhaps it's just me over-anthropomorphizing, but I'd hate to think what it would be like to be sliced and cut, even if I didn't have any actual nerves. So, if for no other reason than to gratify myself, I perform a "sleep" ritual on each part, sort of a spiritual anesthesia.

First I lay it out on the floor; if it's leather or fur I make it lie as flat as possible, with no wrinkles or kinks. I then run my hands over the piece (if it's a full hide from nose to tail) about a foot above it along the entire length. The second time is the same except I lower my hands a few inches, repeating the process until I am stroking the surface itself. With each pass I visualize the energy getting lower and less active. The final time I run my hands down while pressing firmly, pushing the energy down. I then raise my hands and push down on the piece, visualizing pushing the spirit down through the floor, deep into the earth, into a special cavern I've created just for the animal spirits to rest. I place the spirit there and lull it to sleep until I call on it again (when the project is finished).

Occasionally I'll run across a piece of hide or bone or some other thing that has a spirit that wishes to be released from its container. Usually I'll explain to hir what options s/he has if s/he stays, but if s/he insists, I comply with hir wishes.

The method I use is a very simple concept. Once I have performed the aforementioned calming rite, I literally reach down and pull the spirit off of the piece. It usually appears in my mind's eye as the entire animal itself, and I have a tendency to grasp hold of hir by the back of the jawbone–probably a way to "lead" the spirit out of the piece. I then gently set hir down and let hir go hir way, assuring hir that if s/he wishes to hang around my home s/he's more than welcome.

This process may also be used to transfer the residue of the animal from one part to another. At one time I had four separate wolf hides I danced in. Due to time and space issues I found it necessary to streamline my possessions. I didn't want to lose the valuable allies I had in my wolves, but I needed the room desperately. I had one wolf that I danced in most frequently that I chose to keep. I laid all four skins out on the floor of my ritual area and, one by one, I drew the spirit from the other three wolves and placed them into the fourth. This way I was still able to work with all four wolves in spirit but in a manner that allowed for my physical situation at the time.

The purification process isn't just for the animal spirits. It's for me, too. Just before Samhein 2005, I began working with Anubis in order to improve my work with the remains of dead animals. I evoked him and asked him how I could do this. He set me on the task of speaking to each of the things I'd made from animal parts that I still had in my possession at the time. I was to ask each one to show me hir death in as much sensory detail as possible. It was a daunting task, but I set about it as soon as I finished the ritual. It only took a couple of dance costumes and a sculpture made of deer skulls before I got the point. I needed to have more reverence for the deaths these animals had been through; I'd become too focused on the artistic and business end of my work and had forgotten to an extent about the spiritual aspects inherent in it.

I wasn't "in trouble," so to speak; rather, this was a definite reminder to refocus. So I began. Along with my usual purification process for each piece I made, I include a journey into the deaths of the animal parts involved. I go into a light trance and ask the hide, bone, etc. to show me how it died. I then invoke that memory into myself, reliving the animal's last moments in as much detail as possible. Once I come out again, I literally inhale the energy of the memory out of the animal part and banish it by exhaling it out of my body and out of my home.

I also still periodically visit PETA's website, as they often have graphic depictions of animal cruelty in the fur and meat industries, which again helps me to not become too detached from the reality of where the hides and other parts come from. I've even done a meditation in which I was skinned alive as a way of understanding the horrors some of these animals go through prior to their deaths.

This was probably one of the most intense magical workings I've ever done; I performed it not long after my visit from Anubis. After preparing the ritual area I evoked the death-aspects of the elemental totems–Wolf brought dead trees, Hawk flew in poisoned air, Fox's paw was crushed and bleeding in a trap, and the Bears had their skulls split by axes. I allowed myself to be completely abandoned by my guardians; I even, for the first time in a very long time, lost my Wolf–she retreated deep inside me where this couldn't hurt her. I knew, at the end, that everyone would come back–but at that point I was completely forsaken, utterly human.

I then went to the other room, sat down at the computer, and watched a video on PETA's site of animals being skinned alive[4], my partner Taylor making very sure I watched the whole thing. It was horrifying.

Then the skinning began.

Now, obviously, it wasn't on a physical level. But one thing Taylor is very, very good at is energy work, and he may

4 PETA has a number of videos on their website aimed at shocking people out of patronizing the fur and meat industries. The one I used was at http://www.petatv.com/tvpopup/Prefs.asp?video=fur_farm under the heading "Chinese Fur Farm." Regardless of whether it's actual footage, or staged as has been accused by some of PETA's opponents, it's still effectively horrifying.

as well have been stripping my actual skin from me. I allowed
him to use my own ritual knife to slice the "skin" from my body,
then peel it back and pull it off, tossing my remains back to the
floor as he finished with each section. When it was done, he left
me there, "bleeding" on the floor; Taylor even noted that my
physical skin flushed bright red. It was horrible. I had *nothing*
left.

I went into symbolic death. Anubis came to me, then.
He told me to repeat this ritual any time I began losing my
focus. He told me in addition to the rituals I always do, I was to
do an honoring ritual to the animals on every new moon and at
Samhein, and that Taylor would help me remember. There was
no note of punishment in this, only reminding and refocusing.
I'd done no wrong, only lost my focus. In fact, it was a
completely neutral thing.

When I came back out, Taylor healed me, gave me my
energetic skin back, and my physical skin returned to its normal
color. All those who'd showed up for the ritual on the
nonphysical side of things came closer, aiding where they
would. There was a sense of joy and relief that I'd come back
from the Underworld, from my own death. The ritual had done
its job; they'd not wanted to lose me for good.

Now I am hyperaware of the deaths. It will most likely
fade some, but not to the extent it did before. If it does, then I
will repeat this as many times as necessary to make it work.

Putting Them to Work

Now that you've purified the animal parts it's time to make use of them. Take time to ask the parts what they would like to become, if they have any ideas or would like to make suggestions.

Magical tools are always a popular choice. Antler and bone handled knives, rattles, ritual jewelry, fur and leather pouches for other tools and magical items, dance costumes–the possibilities are myriad.

Sometimes the parts don't even need to be altered. Skulls, for instance, make excellent scrying tools. Hold the skull so that you are peering into the hole at its base where the vertebrae attach. You can either do divination for a particular query or use the opportunity to communicate with the spirit of the animal. Skulls have a particularly strong vibe as they have housed the central nervous system–and therefore the center of consciousness.

Dance costumes made from animal parts are excellent tools for invocation. They offer a stronger sympathetic bond to the animal spirit you are invoking, and also allow the residue specific to the components a chance to essentially have a body again. This creates more cooperation among all participants in the ritual and gives the practitioner an opportunity to feel what it is to be that animal. Full or partial pelts work quite well for this.

Animal parts make excellent components of altars and shrines. They may represent the animals themselves, totems, deity forms or whatever beings or energies correspond with the specific species. They add a wild energy to any ritual area.

One of the most dramatic forms of magic I've worked with animal parts has been totem-dancing. One example is my wolf dancing. I first obtained the pelt in Missouri and held onto him for a couple of years after I moved to Pittsburgh. One day he finally decided to tell me what he wanted to be. I'd never created a dance costume before, but he directed me in how to prepare him and wear him. It just so happened that he wrapped around my body perfectly–my arms even fit neatly into the holes where his forelegs had been.

Since then we've danced together numerous times, him enjoying riding a body again and me getting the benefit of seeing through lupine eyes and moving with a wolf's grace. Obviously it took some practice, and I observed the movement of live wolves to get a better idea of how to translate that into my own dancing. I've found that this dancing is not only one of the most effective ways for me to attain a mental and energetic shapeshift, but it's also a great icebreaker with other magical practitioners, too! Occasionally someone will make the mistake of petting the fur while I'm tranced out, which gives me a nasty shock, but for the most part people are respectful and just want to know more about the dance and the wolf himself.

Once I learned the basics from the wolfskin, I began

dancing other animals. The more I practiced, the easier it became to allow that energy to flow into me and to share my own energy. With practice I and whatever animal I danced were able to add our own combined energies into the ebb and flow of the drum circle, increasing the wild nature of the dance.

You don't need an entire pelt to dance an animal, however. I've seen people dance Deer with a pair of antlers, or Bear with a single claw. It's all a matter of what's available to you and how you utilize it.

I've also used animal parts as bases for servitors (magical entities I created). My first servitor, Murray, was made from a dog vertebra.I gave him a clay eyeball, painted him green with blue spots and added a toothy grin across his "face". I used him for repeated tasks and, true to his doggy nature, he did well on a reward basis. Unfortunately I neglected to punish him for not completing tasks properly, and he began to get lazy, much like an intelligent dog figures out how much s/he can get away with. Thus it is that even when we don't intend it, the energy of the animal parts affects our magic.

Some Random Practical Points

Deerskin makes the absolute best leather lacing. It's strong, stretchy and somewhat waterproof, plus it has this lovely sweet scent to it. It's also quite soft and touchable. The easiest way to get the most lacing out of a piece of leather, even if it's a scrap only a few inches square, is to start cutting it into a spiral shape starting from the outside edge. Keep cutting around and around the edge in a continuous piece until you have a long enough piece of lacing.

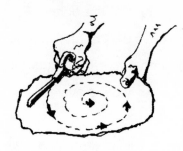

Always have at least two of each item you use frequently. I have on hand at least two each of scissors, Exacto blades, craft glue and rolls of artificial sinew. Be sure that you stock up on oft-used items so you don't you run out of them.

Save your scraps. You never know when you—or someone else—will need them. They make excellent poppet stuffing—just don't give the poppet to anyone with a tendency towards allergies! The absolute smallest bits can be offered to songbirds in the spring as materials for nesting.

Sometimes it's tough to tell real fur or wool yarn from synthetic. If you can obtain a tiny portion of the article in question, put it to the following test: light it on fire. If it burns and smells like burnt hair, it's real. If it melts and smells like burnt plastic, it's fake.

Fur pelts need to be cared for over the years. Every three to five years—or whenever the hide seems to be getting a bit dry—treat the skin (nonfurry) side of the pelt with some mink oil

(I prefer the cream form to the messier liquid.) Don't forget the nose and other exposed skin, as well as the thin strip of skin down the center of the underside of the tail. Vacuum the hide once or twice a year to remove dust and loose hair. Avoid getting the pelt wet if at all possible, though if something more substantial than dust gets on the pelt, a quick bath in water won't hurt hir if s/he's hung out to dry immediately thereafter.

Leather also benefits from mink oil now and then, though be forewarned that it can darken the color of the skin. Claws and turtle shells that still have their scales can be shellacked or coated in clear nail polish to preserve the outer shell. Split or hollow teeth may be filled in with clear epoxy–you can mix in some flour if you'd prefer a white filling. Just be aware that it's a very messy process and you may need to do some cleanup to the teeth afterwards. Gentle application of sandpaper works well.

Bones also require special care, especially if scavenged. If you're fortunate enough to have a private piece of property where bones won't be disturbed, leave them outside for a few weeks. Otherwise if there's still some meat on them, get a large stew pot that will not be used for food again. Boil the bones in water until the flesh becomes soft, then peel it off (don't forget rubber gloves!). Next, soak the bones for one to two days in a 50-50 mix of bleach and water (though be aware that bleach may weaken thinner bones). Any remaining residue may be sanded off. Check skulls and jaws for loose teeth, and glue them in if so desired. More delicate bones like bird skulls that only have a small amount of degradable material on them can be soaked in hydrogen peroxide overnight (make sure you put a lid on it.)

When collecting feathers, place them in a sealable bag and throw them in the freezer for a few weeks to kill off any parasites. Whole wings may be preserved folded or extended. Take a shallow, wide box such as the type that department stores often wrap garments in. Pour a □" layer of Borax in the bottom. Next arrange the wing on top of the Borax however you like. If you're having trouble getting it to stay put, get some small pieces of styrofoam and bury them partially in the Borax. Then take straight pins and pin the wing to the styrofoam. Finally, cover the wing with more Borax and leave for a month. The Borax acts as a dessicant and preserves the wing nicely.

If feathers become mussed, wet them and simply run your fingers up the edge of the feather from the bottom to the top, then lay carefully to dry. This should only be done with individual feathers, as whole wings may become moldy.

Ears on pelts tend to be all squished from the tanning process. They can be easily fixed. First, soak the head in cold water until the ears are soft—usually this takes no more than a half an hour, but check every five to ten minutes. Once it's ready, wring it out until it stops dripping. Lay the skin flat in a place where it won't be disturbed and where it can dry easily. Next, gently pry open the ears until they are as close to a natural position as possible. Fill the ears with small wads of newspaper, molding the skin around the paper until you're satisfied with how the ears look.

Get some thin cord–artificial sinew or twine both work well. Carefully wrap it around the ears to hold everything in place, but not so much that you crush the ears. I've also used paper clips to hold the eartips up as they have a tendency to curl downward. Just clip over the tip of the ear with the longer side pushing against the direction the ear wants to curl.

It usually only takes two to three days for the ears to dry properly. This method can also be used on muzzles that have been scrunched up. Just make sure that you remove the paper after three days to avoid mildew. If it's still a little damp, that's fine, just so long as it will hold its shape.

If you'd like an introductory exercise with which to utilize the information in this chapter, please turn to Appendix C for directions on how to make a fur pouch.

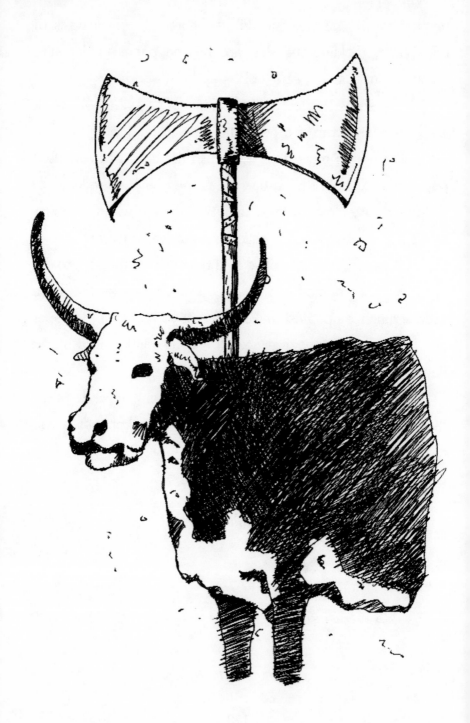

Chapter 7
Animal Sacrifice

Disclaimer: *This chapter is included primarily to complete this book as a treatise on animal magic in all of its forms. The authors and publisher of this chapter take no responsibility for anyone's actions but their own, including any action purportedly caused by someone reading this chapter. In short, any magician worth hir salt can damned well make hir own decisions in regards to ethics and actions. It is not our responsibility to make those decisions for you, just as it's not our responsibility to wipe your ass for you.*

The ritual and magical killing of animals, as well as the offering of their remains to nonhuman entities, is a paleopagan practice that most modern magical practitioners have declined to adopt. Many cite animal rights and humane behavior, though legality also becomes an issue, which Nicholas Graham will discuss later in this chapter.

No matter how highly venerated, animals still meet death at the hands of humans. For example, "Malawians do not make a categorical distinction between the spiritual (unseen) and material aspects of life, and the natural world is viewed as consisting of real entities, with inherent powers and

175

potentialities...[but they] express a consistent anthropocentric or pragmatic attitude towards the natural world, but this, it is important to stress, does not imply an ethic of domination" (The Power of Animals — 1998/*Morris*/p. 6). Therefore, while the qualities of a prey animal may be worked into a culture's group ethic, that prey animal is still food, and food is necessary for life. Hunter-gatherer cultures in particular could not afford prohibitions on certain animals except with great rarity. It was only with the advancement of herding and agrarian societies that such taboos could be created and enforced, the dietary restrictions of Hebrew tradition being a good example.

Once a society shifted from hunter-gatherer status to a more agrarian structure, animal sacrifice tended to replace the rituals formerly used to attract game and appease the higher powers associated therewith. Domesticated animals often weren't considered to be under an Animal Master, but were sometimes sacrificed to more general fertility and agriculture deities. Since domestication made sacrificial beasts easier to procure, the use of sacrifice spread beyond the more traditional reasons, particularly in cultures that found themselves with economic surpluses.

The Romans were quite fond of animal sacrifices and integrated them into many of the celebrations and rituals that occurred on almost a daily basis. Sacrifices were used for offerings, augury, and war and fertility magics, among other purposes. They were a regular occurrence at weddings, appointments to office and celebrations of just about every deity in the massive Roman pantheon.

If an offering for a god was done, the animal had to be chosen according to species, sex, and, frequently, physical traits. The method of slaughter often consisted of stunning then stabbing the animal, and allowing the blood to drain into a vessel. The body was then prepared with different portions allotted to specific purposes. Innards generally were read for divinatory purposes, while the meat was made into a post-ritual feast; whatever was leftover ended up a burnt offering (The Dictionary of Roman Religion — 1996/*Adkins and Adkins*/p. 196-7).

Ancient Hebrew tradition dictated animal sacrifices be made for certain events and atonements as well. In fact the major part of the book of Leviticus–a writing held sacred by both Jews and Christians–details what sorts of sacrifices to make and explicit details on carrying them out.

For instance, an individual guilty of committing an inadvertent sin sometimes later discovered his error (Leviticus, like many of the law books in the bible, addresses only men in the patriarchal society in which it was written). Upon this discovery the man would "bring an unblemished female [lamb]. Having laid his hand on its head, he shall slaughter this sin offering in the place where the holocausts are slaughtered. The priest shall then take some of the blood of the sin offering and put it on the horns of the altar of holocausts. The rest of the blood he shall pour out at the base of the altar. All the fat shall be removed...and the priest shall burn it on the altar..." (Lev. 5 32-35.).

Really makes you wonder about those Biblical literalists, doesn't it?

Scandinavian pagans also had a tradition of animal sacrifice. Horses in particular were favored offerings, and many equine skeletons have been found in peat bogs known to have been receptacles for gifts to the divine. Animals (as well as humans) were also ritually slaughtered and then hung from trees: "[A]s late as the eleventh century there is an account in the history of Adam of Bremen of bodies of men and animals seen dangling from trees in the sacred grove at Uppsala [Sweden]" (Scandinavian Mythology — 1969/Davidson/p. 33).

On the other side of the Atlantic, some indigenous cultures also slew animals for ritual purposes. Jezabel, a friend of mine who is a sixth-generation Hunkpapa Lakhota medicine woman, states that:

Heyokas (sacred clowns/fools) perform a sacrifice of a dog for the Thunder Dreamers Ceremony and the Cleansing Ceremony...They are used to honor the Thunder Beings, bring the Heyokas power, and to help heal people who are in overwhelming suffering and sickness. The dog chosen, however, has to be healthy, strong, obedient, and of good spirit or the ceremony would be weak and the Thunder Beings could possibly take offense. The dog is boiled and the Heyokas reach in the boiling pot bare-handed and eat some of its flesh as well as offer some to each of the sick in the Cleansing Ceremony. (Jezabal, personal communication, 6 June 2005)

This is further elaborated upon in Neihardt's *Black Elk Speaks*:

Then the dog had to be killed quickly and without making any scar, as lightning kills, for it is the power of the lightning that the heyokas have...Then two heyokas tied a slip noose in the rope and put this over the neck of the dog. Three times they pulled the rope gently, one at each end of the rope, and the fourth time they jerked it hard, breaking the neck....Then Wachpanne [the master of the individual ceremony described] singed the dog and washed it well, and after that he cut away everything but the head, the spine and the tail...he threw it so that it fell head first into the boiling water. Then he took the heart of the dog and did with it just what he did with the head and the spine. (Black Elk Speaks — 1972/Neihardt/p.160-161)

Modern-Day Animal Sacrifice

A handful of Northern-tradition heathens carry on the practice of their forebears. The same goes for many of the Afro-Caribbean religions such as Voodoo and Santeria, and a small section of practicing ceremonial magicians following certain grimoire-based rituals. The kosher slaughter of animals for Jewish consumption also still falls under the realm of ritual death.

The stigma against animal sacrifice stems in great part from Christianity's dominance in Western culture. The practice was obviously heathen (never mind the Hebrew traditions and the biblical directions), so sacrifices were demonized along with many other paleopagan practices. As Western societies became progressively more secular other reasons had to be used to uphold the ban. Animal welfare has since become the greatest argument against the practice.

Every now and then some newspaper or another will run an article on a lurid "Satanic animal sacrifice" that occurred in a local cemetery or wooded lot. Generally there will have been someone's household pet cruelly beaten, skinned or burned, with parts removed, all described in graphic detail. It's gotten to the point where animal shelters won't adopt out black cats the month before Halloween for fear that roving bands of demon-worshipping teenagers will slaughter them.

This isn't to say that these events of true cruelty don't happen. They are not the acts of legitimate magical practitioners, however. In all modern examples, great care is paid to the animal to be sacrificed. After all, few entities would want to receive an abused–and therefore flawed–gift. In her article "Hoof and Horn: Animal Sacrifice in Modern Heathen Practice," Galina Krasskova states "Every heathen I interviewed emphasized the sanctity of the sacrificial blot and expressed the preference that no sacrifice be offered, if it could not be offered properly." (Hoof and Horn: Animal Sacrifice in Modern Heathen Practice - 2005/*Krasskova*/p. 25).

For some, the sacrifice is practical on more than just the magical level. The basis for sacrifice in Afro-Caribbean religions revolves around everyday survival. "Food is in short supply in Haiti [the birthplace of Voodoo]. Thus, the sacrifice serves two purposes. It shows the *lwa* how much their followers honor them by giving them something of real value. And it enables the entire *socyete* to share the food of a community, as everyone who attends the ritual joins in the feast" (The Idiot's Guide to Voodoo — 2002/*Turlington*/p. 181-182).

Granted, most magical practitioners aren't living hand-to-mouth during most, if not all, of their earthly life. Very few raise livestock at all, even something so small as an urban hutch of rabbits. In fact, the majority of us reside in cultures in which meat is a bloodless lump of food wrapped in styrofoam and plastic wrap to be reheated by artificial means and possibly seasoned to the point where its original taste is lost. Some cite animal sacrifice as a way to remind ourselves of the reality of death and our part in it. Even if you never kill a single animal in your life, it's worth the experience to tour a slaughterhouse to see just where those spare ribs are coming from. A lot of people are shocked the first time they find out that veal calves spend their brief lives locked in a pen barely big enough to move around in, and that ducks raised for their livers are often force-fed meal–but such is the current state of affairs.

Unlike the commercial meat industry, the death in an animal sacrifice is as quick and painless as possible. For the most part the animal sacrificed becomes a meal for the participants–nothing goes to waste. Some may be burned or otherwise offered to the entity or entities being honored or dealt with, but nothing just gets left to rot once the life has been extinguished.

Other obstacles prevent most practitioners from utilizing animal sacrifice beyond personal moral decisions. Legal barriers, actual or perceived, dissuade most of them. The majority of magicians don't have adequate space or resources to raise the livestock animals traditionally associated with sacrifices, though some get around this by offering smaller animals such as rodents, reptiles, fish and other pet animals. And there is the condemnation that will almost certainly be visited upon them by other magicians if they should happen to mention the practice, to say nothing of the uproar if members of the general public uncover the act.

So why practice animal sacrifice at all? As mentioned previously, it can be a way to reintegrate the death section of the life-death-rebirth cycle into one's practice. In addition, some entities may request at least a small sacrifice as payment for services rendered.

My one experience with animal sacrifice was just such a

thing. One summer I lived in a house in a fairly rural area. Predictably we had a bit of a mouse problem. The cats did what they could, but there were just too many hiding places in the walls. I was concerned for the health of both certain of my ritual tools and the kitchen area in general so I purchased several glue traps and baited them with peanut butter. I created a sigil to enhance the effectiveness of the traps and then asked Bast for her aid in sealing the magic. In return I promised to offer each mouse caught to her.

Within less than twenty-four hours I had my first catch. There was, of course, no way to safely extricate the still-live mouse from the trap—even if I had he'd just have come back to the house. So in an offering to Bast I quickly beheaded hir with a sharp knife; almost immediately a ghostly white cat appeared in my mind's eye to feed on the draining energy.

Irresponsibly, I left the traps out and neglected to check them for several days. I happened to see the one in the closet at one point. There, stuck to the trap, was the corpse of a mouse that had probably dehydrated to death. Bast came to me and said, "This is an unacceptable offering. I want no suffering in this manner. Do not allow this happen again if you wish to continue to work with me." I haven't forgotten since.

There are other ways in which animal sacrifice may be worked into everyday life without compromising any legal issues or raising too many eyebrows. While I don't recommend feeding snakes live food (as the prey can injure the snake in self-defense) there is the occasional reptile that simply will not take pre-killed food. In that case the prey may be offered to a reptile-based entity with the snake as the vehicle. Or if you are one of the few people who raises or hunts hir own food, offer each animal killed to a deity or other entity. You may even wish to create your own ritual to be used each time. Just keep in mind that traditionally the animal sacrificed is viewed with much honor and reverence, rather than just a source of magical energy.

Obviously, too, you can't just go and steal someone's beloved pet for your sacrifice. Regardless of the considerable legal and ethical concerns thereof, it's rather counterproductive to offer up a gift that was never yours in the first place.

The decision to use animal sacrifice is, as with all other magical practices, a personal one. Is it worth the effort to purchase or raise an animal, properly care for it until the time has come to sacrifice it, and then ensure that the death is clean? (For details on proper live animal care, please refer to Chapter 2.) Are there other sacrifices that may be made instead? Can you perform the ritual without being discovered by someone who may make your life much more inconvenient because of it?

Jezabel presents another possible drawback: "I also would recommend that those who do grow attached to animals easily to not raise their sacrificial animals, I can almost guarantee when the time comes that they will not be able to kill it or if they do, will be overcome with grief from loss of the animal's companionship." (Jezabel, personal communication, 6 June 2005)

One little-known backlash that can occur from using death as a mean of magic is illustrated pointedly by Stephen Mace. He relates the story of Flavius Claudius Julianus, the last openly pagan emperor of Rome. Julian's story, which traced his amazing climb up through political and military battlefields, ends with a sudden crash into his own death. This story is punctuated by literally thousands upon thousands of animal sacrifices, the energy of which he poured into magical workings towards his own gain. His downfall came once he'd crossed the threshold into being so drunk on the "vital force" released from each sacrifice that he used his momentum, despite the worst of omens, to charge right into his own demise. The moral of the story? Animal sacrifice is serious magic, and it's very easy to become intoxicated by it. Use with caution. (Nemesis and Other Essays — 1998/*Mace*/p. 20-39)

As with any magical act, particularly the controversial, the decision over animal sacrifice is an intensely personal one that due to its nature and complexity requires consideration of a number of points. Of all forms of animal magic it is perhaps the one to be taken least lightly, as the taking of a life not only releases a large amount of energy but can also have immense psychological repercussions if the practitioner is not fully prepared for the act.

I now turn the figurative podium over to my friend and

fellow magician, Nicholas Graham, for further delineation of the topic.

The Ritual Sacrifice of Animals by Nicholas Graham

Additional Disclaimer: *While Lupa's disclaimer covered things pretty well, I feel the need to include my own disclaimer, in my own words. In magic, you must always re-teach yourself how to leave your expectations behind you. This goes just as much for questions or morality; you cannot judge the morality of a situation until you are presented with it, for until then you haven't enough experience. Right and wrong can only be determined on a case-by-case basis, and what is the highest good one moment may become the most malicious evil in the next. Keep your mind open in all things, and listen to your intuition. Some things mentioned herein are illegal in the United States, and many other areas of the world. Lupa, myself, and the publisher are not liable or responsible for any conscious decisions which the reader makes, or the outcome thereof. Just, please, don't be stupid.*

Legality

Before anything else, I'm going to cover the legality of animal sacrifice. The way I see it, this is going to be the greatest deterrent to the intrepid magician who may wish to experiment in this area.

Most people, when they think on it, begin with the assumption that animal sacrifice is a criminal act in the United States. This is a natural assumption, due to the various animal rights laws now being enacted (many of which have been a long time in coming!), and the current mainstream and fundamentalist religious attitudes holding sway over the minds of many. The fact is, however, that animal sacrifice is perfectly legal under the authority of the Supreme Court. It was never a big legal issue until the Church of the Lukumi Babalu Aye in Hialeah, Florida came along.

In the early 1990s, the Church began the process of opening a Santeria cultural center in Hialeah. They hoped to make it more than a center of worship, but also a social center, a learning center and a place to hold festivals. In response to these efforts, the city of Hialeah passed a number of ordinances against animal sacrifice, or any killing of an animal done without food as its main goal. Thus, religious ritual sacrifice would be criminal, while clubbing a cow to death would be a-okay.

The ordinances passed in Hialeah, but the Church fought. It went all the way to the Supreme Court, in fact, who found in favor of them. The court was unanimous in its decision that the city ordinances were invalid, as they directly contradicted the First Amendment rights to freely practice their religion.[5] Justice Anthony Kennedy was quoted as saying, "Although the practice of animal sacrifice may seem abhorrent to some, religious belief need not be acceptable, logical, consistent, or comprehensible to others in order to merit First Amendment protection." Based upon this court case, anybody who chooses to practice animal sacrifice within a spiritual context could easily argue religious rights in court, and site Church of Lukumi Babalu Aye v. City of Hialeah, 508 U.S. 520 from the year 1993.

As a related note, a number of mainstream religious groups came to the defense of the Church, including several Jewish organizations, the Presbyterian Church and the National Association of Evangelicals. It seems that nobody wants to see religious rights revoked for, having done it for one group, any religious group becomes vulnerable. For this effort, all organizations involved deserve our thanks.

---

[5] Full details on the case can be found at
http://caselaw.lp.findlaw.com/scripts/getcase.pl?navby=search&friend=<%FRIEND%>&linkurl=<%LINKURL%>&graphurl=<%GRAPHURL%>&court=US&case=/data/us/508/520.html and a summary can be found at
http://religiousfreedom.lib.virginia.edu/court/luku_v_hail.html.
A wonderful introduction to Santeria, as well as information concerning this court case, can be found at http://religiousmovements.lib.virginia.edu/nrms/santeria.html.

[Lupa's note: Just keep in mind that local authorities aren't likely to respect the aforementioned court case. If they want to arrest you they'll come up with a reason. I now return you to Nick.]

Theory

The theory of ritual sacrifice is the idea of mutual benefit; some might compare it to a form of spiritual free market exchange. A spirit of some form agrees to give one service in exchange for another. In more traditionally religious systems (such as Greek and Roman paganism), the human agrees to perform a service in the hopes that a god will be convinced to aid him.

The question is invariably asked, why do these spirits (gods included) need anything from humans at all? Aren't they closer to infinity than humanity and, thus, more able to provide for themselves anything which they might require? Isn't it absurd to think that they require anything at all?

The simplest answer is that these spiritual forces are not entirely non-physical. To medieval Muslims, demons (called *Djinni*, or *genie*) were composed of the purest fire; to the Greek and Roman magicians, they (called *daimones* or *genius*, by those respective cultures) were thought to be composed of the most rarefied air (*aer*). Either way, these substances, while purer than their mundane counterparts, are still material in a way that would allow direct contact between these spiritual agencies and

189

the physical world. Having bodies, even if they're loose bodies invisible to our gelatinous sensory orbs, they are still bodies and, thus, require nourishment and care. How do most humans acquire their required nourishment? Through trade, of course! And so it is with the *Djinni*, faerie and Spirits of the Air.

What's more, they don't seem to absolutely require this nourishment or, at least, they don't appear to require it nearly as often as humans do. Additionally, they are nourished equally by things of the body, of the mind, and of the spirit. Each such being has its own tastes and preferences, just as a human or other sentient animal might. Many of the Loa of Voodoo, for instance, greatly enjoy rum, a fine cigar or goat meat; the Hindu God Ganesha loves milk and honey; many demons of the European tradition equally enjoy fine art, powerful poetry or a delicious steak dinner; the Judeo-Islamic-Christian God seems to enjoy burnt lambs or to sup on the flesh of his only son. As S. Jason Black and Christopher S. Hyatt pointed out in their incredible manual of demonic evocation, *Pacts With the Devil*, any way you look at it, damned souls are a-dime-a-dozen, so there's no need to trade for such a common commodity when there are more interesting and nourishing things to be gained.

Practice

This section will only be of interest to a small number of readers, as I realize that not many people who call themselves 'pagans' and 'magicians' agree with these methods. The practice of the ritual sacrifice is a simple one, and I will give several alternatives for those who don't wish to kill animals with their own hands.

One of the biggest problems with animal sacrifice that most people have is that of cruelty; won't the animal feel more pain at the hands of a magician wielding a knife than at the hands of a trained executioner such as work in slaughterhouses? The simple truth is no. Animals (both for fur and food) suffer far more in the slaughterhouse; broken legs while walking down ramps, yet they're forced to keep going; having electrodes shoved into their rectums and not being killed on the first shock; failed attempts at severing or crushing their heads which cause intense pain and distress, but do not kill on the first or even second blow. No, this is not a humane way of obtaining food. Isn't a swift, clean death far preferable? This is the way a magician would do it. Animal torture has never been part of the sacrifice. After all, ignoring any questions of cruelty, who would want a battered and broken gift in exchange for services rendered? The quickest, most painless methods available to the modern magician for the killing of a sacrifice is slitting the throat of the animal with a very sharp knife (especially for larger animals), or swiftly, cleanly breaking the neck (for smaller animals).

Of course, there are always specific ways of presenting the sacrifice after the animal has been killed. For the Hebrews, it involved slitting the animal's throat over a stone altar, removing the organs and burning the carcass. Similarly, the Romans would kill the animal upon an altar and eviscerate it; they would then 'read' the innards for divinations of upcoming important events, such as wars or the health of important figures. Typically, in Voodoo and Santeria, the sacrificed animal is cooked and eaten by the community, perhaps with part of it set aside for the spirit to which it was sacrificed. If you're working within a specific tradition, or out of a particular manual of magic, you should have a pretty good idea of how to deal with the sacrifice. I'd like to add here, however, that I try hard to get close to the spirit of the Santeria and Voodoo practitioners in my own work. Even if my sacrifice is a fine *filet mignon* purchased from my local butcher, I try to find a way to share it. The last time, for example, I purchased three *filet* cuts; the first cut was the sacrifice, the second cut was for me, and the last cut I gave to a good friend.

Similar to the concern of how to kill and present the sacrifice is the question of knowing just which type of animal, and which animal specifically, to use. Many traditions of magic and religion will tell you in their literature what type of animal to be used for different purposes. Similarly, most grimoires will specify things like a black cock or a virgin goat, for instance. If your source does not specify for you, or if there's any doubt between several options, you may always perform your preferred form of divination to figure it out. First, perform a prayer to the appropriate deity, then do your divination. Any divinatory method with which you're relatively accurate and detailed will be good. The same goes for figuring out which specific animal to use. Before resorting to divination, however, make sure that the animal to which you have access is healthy and uninjured. The nicer the coat of fur (or scales, or skin), the better. Make sure that the animal is, in general, a good example of its species. That alone should be good enough, but if you have multiple similar options, you may consider divination as a solution. As a final note on this topic, you might remember that the Romans considered it a 'bad omen' if the animal to be sacrificed turned away from the site of sacrifice while being led there. That's culturally specific, of course, so feel free to use it or ignore it, according to your intuition.

I've also been asked how to determine if an animal's spirit is willing to be the sacrifice. Honestly, I don't put much stock in this, because most animals aren't terribly willing to be killed and eaten by anyone or anything, so why should gods and demons make any difference compared to other predators? If this is important to you, I suggest that you simply avoid animal sacrifice altogether, or find your own methods, though I honestly consider any such methods (short of the animal actually learning to speak in order to tell you) to be suspect, at best.

Now on to the topic of alternatives. If you do not want to kill animals in your own rituals, but would like to make use of the powerful technique of sacrifice, you can look into many other options. Purchasing an appropriate cut of meat (*filet mignon*, beef heart, and beef liver are often good choices) can work quite well. Other consumables, such as good liquor, fine wine, gourmet candies and various other drugs (tobacco, marijuana, mushrooms, and so on, depending upon your willingness and ability to get them) will also present themselves as options.

Beyond consumables of various sorts, other sacrifices are possible in the form of creative effort and magical activity. Poetry about the spirit involved, a painting of the spirit, or a small shrine for them, for instance. There are many more possibilities than could be set down here; the most important thing to remember is that you perform a divination of some sort (Tarot, Ouija or a pendulum work particularly well, as they can give very detailed responses) in order to be sure that your sacrifice will be acceptable. After all, there's really nothing less fun than an angry god or demon.

Conclusion

I find that sacrifice is an indispensable aspect of any form of magic that deals with gods or spirits of any sort. Of course, this is nothing more or less than my opinion, based on my own experience. I feel that I've given a fair amount of instruction on how to make use of it in your own system of magic, without being forced to cross any moral borders that you might have. In the end, it's your decision, and I wish you all the luck in the world in your efforts for self-development. We're all in this together.

Note: *Again, we reiterate that neither the authors nor the publisher of this chapter are in any way responsible for any acts of stupidity or cruelty performed by those who read this book. Remember—sacrificial animals are well cared for and their deaths are as painless as possible, usually more humane than that of the cow that became the burger on your plate! Any decision you make in regards to this or any other issue ought to be made with care and much thought, and is your responsibility alone!*

Afterword

I realize that my tone in this book has been one primarily of functionality. This is due to my approach of the subject as an experimental magician–one who is interested in the practicality and flexibility of any given paradigm.

I don't want to leave the reader with the idea that animal magic is purely a path of function. On the contrary, its form is a breathtaking thing, from the radical mental shift of a full-on totemic invocation to the simple pleasures of everyday life with a familiar creature.

I hesitate to define for anyone beside myself just what form the relationship between magician and animal magic will take because, as with any other magical practice, it is an intensely personal journey. For the "buffet-style" Chaote, the bond may be a fleeting, single-ritual agreement that is quickly passed on for the next act. The in-depth totemist may spend an entire lifetime creating a relationship with one particular species. And for some animal magic may simply not be a reality–after all, the key to successful magic is finding the symbols, entities and ceremonies which trigger the shifts in internal and external reality that create the desired changes. Then there are those who may read this book from purely a theoretical, scholarly stance–and that's okay, too.

What I want you, the reader, to come away from this work with is a basic idea of what forms of animal magic exist and some starting points for your own practice. I offer you the basic tools and some ideas for expanding your practice.

The rest, as they say, is all up to you.

To contact Lupa, the author, you may email chaohippie@excite.com or you can contribute to her Livejournal madness at http://lupabitch.livejournal.com. Her website is http://www.thegreenwolf.com.

To contact Nicholas Graham, guest essayist, you may email anituel@gmail.com.

To contact Jim Towns, illustrator, you may email jim@madmonkeyproductions.com.

Appendix A: Guided Totem Meditation

This meditation may be used to find primary or secondary totems. I have had better success using it for secondaries–if you are going to try to determine a primary with it, multiple performances should be done in order to account for any preconceived notions or unclear results. Keep in mind that you may not see any animal at first. If this occurs, give it a few weeks at least and then try again. Some folks aren't ready to meet a particular totem; others may simply need to work with a different set of entities; still others simply don't get much out of guided meditations and visualizations.

You may either record yourself reading this meditation aloud and play it back or have another person read it to you–preferably someone with a pleasant voice. Nothing ruins a good guided meditation like a deadpan monotone with a cold. As with any other meditation, make sure your setting is quiet and undisturbed and that you can get into a comfortable position that may be held for 15-30 minutes but won't cause you to fall asleep in the meantime.

Make your body become completely still. Don't move any part of your body. Concentrate on being entirely motionless. (Allow at least two minutes for this.)

Now breathe as deeply and slowly as you possibly can, in through the nose and out through the mouth. Create an even, steady flow of air. Feel the tension leave your body with each breath. (Minimum three minutes.)

Feel your body sink into the ground beneath you. If there is a manmade floor, feel yourself pass through it and into the cool Earth below. Feel your body become a part of that Earth, solid and unmovable. (One minute.)

Send the upper half of your body high into the sky. Feel the wind rush around you and the clouds brush against your skin. Feel yourself expand into that vast open space and become a part of the Sky. (One minute.)

Now feel yourself being a part of both the Earth and the Sky, solid and vast, and know that as long as the Earth is beneath you and the Sky above you, no harm may come to you on your journey. (One minute.)

Visualize a natural hole–it may be a burrow in the ground, an open knot in a tree, a space amid branches that leads to the sky above, a hole in the ice over Arctic seas. It may be as large as a stone arch or as small as a single cell. See it before you, and enter into it. (One-two minutes.)

Find yourself led down into a long, dark tunnel. You may be running, floating, flying, swimming or crawling through it. (One minute should suffice.)

At the end of the tunnel is another opening. As you pass through this opening, enter into a natural place in which you are very comfortable. It may be a large field, a forest, a snowy plain, a body of water, or the broad sky. Explore this place. Note what the natural flora is, what season and time of day it is and how you move through it. (One-two minutes.)

As you wander this place, you see an animal approaching swiftly. Note what sort of animal it is, how it approaches you, whether it seems to be pleased that you are there or acting aggressively. Pay attention to any specific characteristics such a color, size and sex, and whether it is accompanied by others. Note also if it shifts forms, even into another species entirely. (Two minutes.)

Converse with the animal. Ask it why it is there. If it has acted aggressively, make sure you inquire as to the reason. Find out what the animal has to teach you. Ask how you may strengthen the bond with it. (At least three minutes, preferably five to seven or more if desired.)

It is now time to return to the waking world. Thank the animal for its time and teachings, and promise that you will continue the conversation at a later time. If you wish, gift the animal with a food it likes or other boon. Then turn and go back to the tunnel and return back to the upper world. (At least three minutes.)

As you come back out of the tunnel, start to become aware of your body again. Begin to move slowly, starting with your fingers and toes, then working up your limbs, then your torso and finally your neck and head. Save opening your eyes for last. Don't rush it; give yourself plenty of time to come back to physical reality. (Allow as much time as necessary for this; you don't want to get the mental version of the bends by shocking your system with a quick wake-up.)

Once you've recovered, write or sketch what you saw in as much detail as possible while it's still fresh in your mind. Don't worry if it isn't high-quality art or prose; what matters is that it reminds you as vividly as possible of your experience whenever you reflect upon it.

*I must give Peter J. Carroll a big thank-you for *Liber MMM*, which helped to hone my inhibitory meditation skills and enhanced this particular meditation quite a bit. I also have to thank numerous totemic authors, meditation guides and other folks that I've been able to trade ideas and experiences with for inspirations and idea that went into the creation of this meditation.

Appendix B: Simple Divination Techniques

I am a big fan of using divination to check my work, as it were. The last thing I want is to devolve into a mess of self-justifying delusions and hyperactive imagination. I keep a sharp Occam's Razor in my toolkit.

Divination can be used to get a clarification of an unsure journey, to determine whether or not a magical working was successful when the results aren't easily observed, to communicate with various spirits and, of course, as a focus for predictions. Most people think of the flashier tarot and rune spreads, or even the dreaded ouija board, all of which are excellent for more detailed readings.

Sometimes all you need is a simple "yes" or "no" answer. There are several tools perfect for just such a thing. The pendulum is one of the best-known. Pendulums come in a variety of materials—mine is carved from a lovely piece of amethyst. The important thing is that the pendulum is well balanced and that the cord is long enough to allow clear movement to occur and be observed.

As for the methods of divining answers, the best way is to ask the pendulum itself when you first obtain it. Ask it what motion it uses for a "yes" answer, then allow it to move in that fashion. Check also for the motions for "no" and "maybe/ask more questions."

Everyone carries a divination tool in their pocket–the common coin. I like using a quarter, but anything will work. Just flip the coin and let the side it lands on determine your answer. I like doing a best two-out-of-three series–whichever side comes up twice of three times is my answer.

The Obi are a set of four cola nuts or other flat objects with one side of each painted black, the other white. Stemming from Afro-Caribbean religions, the Obi give a bit more detailed answer than the pendulum or coin, but not so involved and complicated as tarot. The Obi are held in closed-cupped hands and the question is whispered to them; they are them tossed as runes and the way the fall determines the answer.

The meanings that follow are drawn from *Urban Voodoo* by S. Jason Black and Christopher S. Hyatt.

Alafia (Four White): Peace. Quietude. Can denote passive imbalance. If the first throw results in Alafia the Obi must be tossed again.

Etawa (One Black, Three White): Conflict. A battle, minor or major. Confusion. If the first throw results in Etawa the Obi must be tossed again.

Ejife (Two Black, Two White): Balance. "..a harmonious, perfectly functioning situation." (Black and Hyatt 2000, p. 132)

Okana (Three Black, One White): Basically all going as is expected, nothing remarkable. "...the omen of the average day." (Black and Hyatt 2000, p. 132)

Oyekun (Four Black): Negativity. Worst case scenario; time to act to counter the situation. Also may mean an indeterminate answer.

Just about anything can be made into a simple divination tool, really. If you have a familiar or pet with a regular feeding schedule, place three dishes of food down in a row—one for "yes," one for "no" and one for "maybe." Whichever dish the animal goes to first has your answer. Or you can place three slips of paper with the answers on them in a bag and draw one out. For a more long-term query, try planting three seeds—whichever one grows the fastest will be the one to pay attention to.

The possibilities are endless. Use your imagination and find the method that works most consistently for you. Don't think that you have to toss stones or bones or dice every time you have any problem whatsoever—divination is meant to be a tool to be used alongside common sense, planning and hindsight. It's good for catching blind spots in our perception and for clarifying muddy waters.

Appendix C — How to Make a Fur Pouch

For this project you'll need the following:

- Two 5" x 7" rectangles of fur
- Strong thread (I prefer artificial sinew, split down to size if necessary)
- Glover's needles: these are small straight needles with sharp, triangular tips. I recommend the John James brand
- Sharp scissors and/or Exacto knife
- A hard surface that doesn't need to stay pristine
- A sage smudge or other method of purification
- An offering for the spirit of the animal whose fur you use

First, lay the pieces of fur down on your workspace. Gently stroke the energy surrounding the fur several times. Start about twelve inches above it, then lower your hands to four, then two inches, then lightly stroke the fur, feeling the energy lower into the pieces each time. On the final pass run your hands over the fur firmly. Then raise your hands a bit and lower them down onto the fur. Visualize your hands going through the workspace, through the floor, deep into the Earth, taking the spiritual residue of the fur pieces into a safe, dry cavern. Tell the spirits to sleep until you call them again.

Next, layer the two pieces with the skin sides (the sides without hair) on the outside. Trim them until the edges are relatively even. Cut four slits along the top edge of each piece about ¾" from the edge.

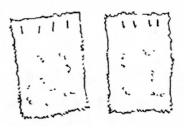

Layer the fur together as before. Thread a needle, making sure to make a sizable knot at one end of the thread. Start at one upper corner and stitch the two pieces together. Restitch at this place three or four times to create a stronger bond as this stitch will have the most stress placed upon it during opening and closing.

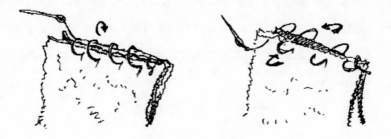

Using either a whipstitch (first picture) or running stitch (second picture), sew the two pieces of fur together, leaving the top open, of course. Repeat the multiple stitches at the opposite top corner. Then stitch all the way back to the beginning to double the strength all around.

Tie off your thread and trim it. Turn the pouch right side out. If all went well, you'll have a furry pouch on both sides.

For the drawstrings, cut six equal length pieces of cord an inch or two longer than you want the final drawstrings to be. Make sure your measurement accounts for the drawstrings passing all the way around the circumference of the pouch's opening, plus at least six inches extra at each end.

Make two braids out of the cord. You can either tie one end to a narrow immobile object such as a dresser knob or tie a knot in one end and sit in a lotus position with the knot clasped between the balls of your feet. This makes braiding infinitely easier. Braid each drawstring, then knot at the other end.

Take one drawstring and weave it through the slits in the pouch. Go in with the first one (make sure it's one closest to the stitching), then out, then in, and so on. Do this all the way around the pouch until you've returned to the slit you started with.

Repeat with the other, only start at the other side of the pouch, so that the ends of the second drawstring are directly opposite the first.

Now for purification. The method of purification isn't so important as the act of purification itself. For instance, I smudge with sagebrush leaves, and make sure every inch of the pouch is touched by the smoke, including the inside. In fact, I'll turn the pouch upside-down, allow it to fill with smoke, then quickly close it. You might say a small prayer over the pouch: "Thank you to [animals whose parts are in the pouch] for contributing to this work. May you be honored and respected for who and what you are." Then make your offering to the spirit(s) whose parts were used in the pouch.

You might want to periodically purify your pouch and make an offering to the spirit if you feel it necessary. Just make sure an initial purification and offering are done before you put the pouch to use.

Appendix D: Recommended Animal-Based Charities

One of the most effective and appreciated offerings you can make to any animal, whether spiritual or not, is to aid the physical members of the species in need. Because of human overpopulation and greed many animals are endangered–some to the point where their population is literally in the dozens. Domestic animals face hardships at the hands of humans, from starvation to abandonment to outright cruelty.

The following organizations work to prevent animal abuse, strive to restore endangered species or otherwise work for the betterment of nonhuman animals. The Defenders of Wildlife, receives 10% of what I make on my artwork. You can donate money to them, or for organizations such as the Humane Society volunteer opportunities abound. Animal shelters in general offer a wide variety of adoptable animals–if you're in the market for a pet of any sort, be it a cat or dog, bird, ferret, rabbit or so forth, check your local shelters before you even consider pet stores. You may be pleasantly surprised!

Feel free to research and contact any of the following organizations. They're all ones I've found to be dedicated and focused in their work, and genuine in their goals.

The Defenders of Wildlife
National Headquarters
1130 17th Street, NW
Washington, DC 20036
USA
(202) 682-9400
info@defenders.org
http://www.defenders.org

The Defenders of Wildlife work to protect wild species, large predators in particular, worldwide. Programs include not only population growth but also habitat preservation and endangerment prevention.

American Society for the Prevention of Cruelty to Animals (ASPCA)
424 E. 92nd Street
New York, NY 10128-6804
USA
(212) 876-7700
information@aspca.org
http://www.aspca.org

Royal Society for the Prevention of Cruelty to Animals (RSPCA)
Wilberforce Way
Southwater
Horsham
West Sussex
RH13 9RS

United Kingdom
0870 75 30 284
http://www.rspca.org.uk

The SPCA in general is aimed primarily towards the welfare of domestic animals, though the various branches do sometimes have campaigns involving wildlife. They do a lot of work towards educating the public about issues and proper domestic animal care.

Humane Society of the United States (HSUS)
2100 L Street, NW
Washington, DC 20037
(202) 452-1100
http://www.hsus.org/

While the Humane Society is best known for pet adoptions, the organization has extensive campaigns for domestic and wild animals alike.

World Wildlife Federation (WWF) International
Avenue du Mont Blanc
CH 1196 Gland
Switzerland
+41 22 364 9111
questions@wwfint.org
http://www.panda.org

One of the best-known wildlife preservation organizations, the World Wildlife Federation has spent the past four decades working with issues on a global scale. They focus a lot on both species and habitat based programs, and include the needs of indigenous cultures in their solutions for worldwide problems.

Glossary of Terms

Anthropomorphize: To assign human qualities or assumptions to nonhuman beings, actions or situations.

Animal sacrifice: A magical ritual in which one or more living animals are killed; the energy from the death is then channeled into the magic. Sacrificial animals, contrary to popular opinion, are extremely well cared for, and the deaths are usually more humane than those met by animals in slaughterhouses, fur farms, etc. Most commonly recognized in, but not limited to, Afro-Caribbean religions such as Santeria.

Aspecting: A process by which certain harmonious sets of personality traits are personified. These personae may then be used as "masks" that the magician wears in order to better understand the traits associated with them.

Biodiversity: Literally, a diversity of life. Biodiversity in context refers to the exceptional variety of life forms, specifically animals, with which we share this world. While species of mammals, birds and other vertebrates usually number in the thousands, the number of individual species of insects is in the millions.

215

Composite species: a species of animal that is a combination of parts and traits of two or more other animals; gryphons, unicorns and the chimera are all examples of composite species.

Cryptozoology: literally, the study of hidden animals. A field of fringe scientific study that involves the classification and search for evidence of unknown species such as the Loch Ness Monster, Bigfoot and the Jersey Devil.

Cultural appropriation: the act of drawing on a particular aspect of a culture one is not a part of and taking it out of context. Generally a negative term, particularly when the culture being taken from is a minority while the culture appropriating is the majority. Cultural appropriation almost always results in the appropriated aspects being significantly changed from their original meaning, often bringing accusations of "watering down".

Evocation: Calling an entity into an area outside the self; an example is the standard work with Goetic demons.

Familiar: A physical animal that aids a magician in ritual work as well as adding to the natural ambience of ritual space and everyday life. More than a pet, a familiar has special qualities adding to hir regular role as a companion animal.

Guided journey (alternatively, guided meditation): A ritual in which a person listens to a structured meditative instruction, either prerecorded or read by another person, which offers the seeker cues to lead hir into a (usually) visual alternate reality for a specific purpose.

Invocation: Calling an entity into the self; or, conversely, immersing the self into the entity; an example is the Wiccan ritual of Drawing Down the Moon.

Neopagan: Literally, "new pagan"; refers to the modern reconstruction of pagan religions, generally from the dawn of Wicca in the 1940's on.

Occam's Razor: A concept solidified by William of Ockham, a medieval scholar; essentially states that the simplest answer is the most likely. In this context, look to the mundane before the magical when attempting to decipher a phenomenon.

Otherkin: A subculture or set of subcultures of people who believe they are something other than human, whether in body or spirit. Includes those who identify as elves, faeries, dragons and other supposedly "mythological" beings, as well as therianthropes and a few other miscellany.

Paleopagan: Literally, "early pagan"; generally refers to pre-Christian pagan religions. May also be use to refer to modern indigenous religions that are relatively complete, such as those of American Indian tribes. As per Bonewits.

Servitor: A nonphysical entity created by a magician for the purpose of performing errands; may be for a single working or may be more permanent.

Sigil: A stylized design or emblem that represents a particular magical desire which can be charged by the magician in a number of manners to achieve the end desired.

Therianthrope: A person who identifies partially or wholly as an animal in a human body. This person has a stronger connection to their animal than simple totemism; where a totem is an external influence; the therianthrope's animal energy is internal.

Totem: In paleopagan terms, generally speaking, an animal spirit or archetype that guards, rules over, or otherwise represents a certain group of people within a culture; often associated with exogamy. In neopagan terms, an animal spirit or archetype that often has a strong bond with an individual practitioner. Totems embody the energy and attributes of an entire species in a manner that humans can understand and communicate with.

Bibliography

Adkins, Lesley and Roy A. Adkins (1996). Dictionary of Roman Religion. New York:
Facts on File, Inc.

Barlowe, Wayne Douglas (1996). Barlowe's Guide to Fantasy: Great Heroes and
Bizarre Beings from Imaginative Literature. New York: HarperCollins.

Black, S. Jason and Christopher S. Hyatt, Ph.D. (1995). Urban Voodoo: A Beginner's
Guide to Afro-Caribbean Magic. Tempe, AZ: New Falcon Publications.

Bonewits, Isaac (2006). Bonewits' Essential Guide to Witchcraft and Wicca. New York:
Citadel Press Books.

Breslaw, Elaine, editor (2000). Witches of the Atlantic World: A Historical Reader and
Primary Sourcebook. New York: New York University Press.

Brown, Joseph Epes (1997). Animals of the Soul: Sacred Animals of the Oglala Sioux.
Rockport, MA: Element Books, Inc.

Bulfinch, Thomas (1981). Bulfinch's Mythology. New York: Dell Publishing Co., Inc.

Campbell, Joseph (1984). The Masks of God: Primitive Mythology. New York: Penguin
Books.

Ceilede (2005). Liber Chromatria: An Exploration of the Eight Selves. Konton Magazine, Volume 2.1 p. 20-22.

Clark, Jerome (1993). Unexplained! 347 Strange Sightings, Incredible Occurrences, and Puzzling Physical Phenomena. Detroit: Visible Ink Press.

Cohn, Norman (2000). The Night-witch in Popular Imagination. In Elaine Breslaw (ed.). Witches of the Atlantic World: A Historical Reader and Primary Sourcebook (117-125). New York: New York University Press.

Crowley, Aleister (1994). Magick Without Tears. Tempe, Arizona: New Falcon Publications.

Cunningham, David Michael, Taylor Ellwood and Amanda R. Wagener (2003). Creating Magical Entities: A Complete Guide to Entity Creation. Perryburg, OH: Egregore Publishing.

Dalton, Michael (2000) Conjuration and Witches. In Elaine Breslaw (ed.). Witches of the Atlantic World: A Historical Reader and Primary Sourcebook. (365-368). New York: New York University Press.

Davidson, H.R. Ellis (1969). Scandinavian Mythology. London: Paul Hamlyn.

Elder, John and Hertha D. Wong (1994). Family of Earth and Sky: Indigenous Tales of Nature from Around the World. Boston: Beacon Press.

Ellwood, Taylor (2004). Pop Culture Magick. Stafford: Immanion Press.

Greene, Rosalyn (2000). The Magic of Shapeshifting. Boston: WeiserBooks.

Harner, Michael (1990). The Way of the Shaman. San Francisco: HarperCollins Pub.

Jakkal (2005). Retrieved April - May, 2005 from http://www.shifters.org.

Jamal, Michele (1995). Deerdancer: The Shapeshifter Archetype in Story and in Trance.
New York: Penguin Books.

Krasskova, Galina (2005). Hoof & Horn: Animal Sacrifice in Modern Heathen Practice.
PanGaia #40, 22-25.

Leach, Maria, and Jerome Fried, editors (1984). Funk & Wagnall's Standard Dictionary
of Folklore, Mythology and Legend. San Francisco: HarperCollins Pub.

Levi-Strauss, Claude (1962). Totemism. Boston: Beacon Press.

Mace, Stephen (1998). Nemesis and Other Essays. Milford, Connecticut: self-published.

Marie de France (1999). The Lais of Marie de France. New York: Penguin Books.

Morris, Brian (1998). The Power of Animals: An Ethnography. Oxford: Berg.

Murray, Grace A. (1996). Ancient Rites and Ceremonies. London: Senate.

Neihardt, John G. (1972). Black Elk Speaks. New York: Pocket Books.

Palmer, Jessica Dawn (2004). Animal Wisdom: The Definitive Guide to the Myth,
Folklore and Medicine Power of Animals. London: Thorsons.

Parker, Arthur C. (1975). The Indian How Book. New York: Dover Publications, Inc.

Ross, Anne and Don Robins (1989). The Life and Death of a Druid Prince. New York:
Touchstone.

Saunders, Nicholas J. (1995). Animal Spirits. Canada: Little, Brown and Co.

Stewart, R.J. Ambassadors to the Animals. PanGaia, Vol. 40 p. 18-21.

Turlington, Shannon R. (2002). The Complete Idiot's Guide to Voodoo. Indianapolis:
Alpha Books.

Wilson, Robert Anton (1983). Prometheus Rising. Phoenix: Falcon Press.

Yolen, Jane, editor (1986). Favorite Folktales From Around the World. New York:
Pantheon Books.

Other Recommended Reading

Andrews, Ted (1993). Animal-Speak. Minneapolis: Llewellyn Publications.

--. (1999). Animal-Wise. Jackson, Tennesee: Dragonhawk Publishing.

Galenorn, Yasmine (2004). Totem Magic. Berkeley: Crossing Press.

Telesco, Patricia and Rowan Hall (2004). Animal Spirit: Spells, Sorcery and Symbols   from the Wild. Franklin Lakes, New Jersey: New Page Books.

Index

Printed in the United States
121356LV00002B/262-288/A